CHILDREN OF
OPEN ADOPTION

Brian

CHILDREN OF OPEN ADOPTION
and their families

Kathleen Silber, M.S.W., A.C.S.W.

Patricia Martinez Dorner, M.A., L.P.C.

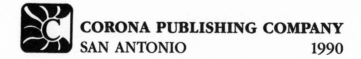

CORONA PUBLISHING COMPANY

SAN ANTONIO   1990

Copyright © 1989 by Kathleen Silber
and Patricia Martinez Dorner

Library of Congress Cataloging-in-Publication Data

Silber, Kathleen, 1943-
    Children of open adoption and their families / Kathleen Silber,
Patricia Martinez Dorner.
        p.   cm.
    Includes bibliographical references.
    ISBN 0-931722-78-0 (pbk.)
    1. Adoption--United States. 2. Children, Adopted--United States.
3. Foster parents--United States.   I. Dorner, Patricia Martinez,
1946-   . II. Title.
HV875.55.S58 1990
362.7'34'0973--dc20
DLC
for Library of Congress   89-85840
                                                              CIP

Book design by Betsy Davis
Printed and bound in the United States of America

10 9 8 7 6 5 4 3 2 1

We dedicate this book to our parents

George and Gilda Younnel
Susan and Joseph L. Martinez

And to our children
Sarah and Erik

* * *

Jennifer and Katherine
And their birthmothers
Gloria and Cindy

ACKNOWLEDGEMENTS

We want to thank all of the adoptive parents, birth-parents, and children who candidly shared their open-adoption experiences. We know it took a lot of time and effort to respond to our questionnaires and to participate in interviews. We hope that the inclusion of their stories will facilitate heightened understanding of the dynamics of open adoption and contribute to making this practice the norm.

We want to recognize all of the individuals who asked for this book to become a reality—the countless adoption professionals and adoptive parents who repeatedly told us of their need to know about the effects of open adoption. Special thanks also go to Alberta Taubert, Sally Gooze, D.L. Click, and Deirdre Patillo for their editing and typing assistance.

Our appreciation goes to our publisher, David Bowen, for his encouragement to make this book a reality and for his continued commitment to the advocacy of open adoption. Finally, we want to thank our husbands, Herb and Fred, for their assistance with their computer expertise, typing, editing, and, most importantly, their support during this project.

Kathleen and Patricia

CONTENTS

Visitation
Infertility Revisited
Discipline

Introduction

In 1982 Kathleen Silber and Phylis Speedlin wrote *Dear Birthmother*, which explored some of the myths in adoption and detailed the evolution of open adoption, from letter exchanges to face-to-face meetings and ongoing contact. *Dear Birthmother* has had a tremendous effect on adoption practice nationwide, resulting in a significant shift from traditional adoption to open adoption. Today most adoption agencies and intermediaries offer at least some components of openness. However, since the publication of *Dear Birthmother*, open adoption has also continued to evolve. This book will examine that evolution, as well as the lifelong impact on all parties, particularly the adopted children.

☐　　☐　　☐

I am Kathleen Silber. At the time I co-authored *Dear Birthmother* I was a Regional Director of an adoption agency in Texas. In the early to mid-seventies when adult adoptees and birthparents "came out of the closet" and spoke of the problems which resulted from traditional adoption, I began to question traditional agency practices and my own professional attitudes. Under my direction, the agency began taking dramatic steps to open up the adoption process. As a result, the agency became a pioneer in the practice of open adoption and consequently a model adoption program nationally.

I left Texas in 1986 and worked for a large adoption agency in California, again practicing open adoption. However,

I quickly discovered that the opportunity for creativity and flexibility which I had enjoyed in Texas did not exist in many California agencies. As in many states, regulation by the state inhibits innovative and responsive services. The laws and regulations governing agencies are based on traditional adoption and have not changed to reflect changes in society. In California, as in many other states, the most progressive services are offered by independent practitioners, not agencies. As a result I no longer advocate agency adoption. Instead, I advocate open adoption, with professional counseling, support, and education. Since 1988 I have worked for a nonprofit independent, open-adoption organization which offers these essential ingredients. This is an alternative to both conventional agency adoption and conventional independent adoption.

Since *Dear Birthmother* I have also evolved in my thinking about open adoption. I am more committed than ever to this practice, which is truly more responsive to people's needs, as well as more honest and humane. I have personally been involved with several hundred open adoptions, and I have observed that they include a lot of love and caring, rather than the fear and mystery which have traditionally surrounded adoption. As a result of my experiences, I advocate meeting in person, sharing full identifying information, and engaging in ongoing contact over the years (either through correspondence or in person). I think it is preferable for all parties to have direct access to ongoing contact and to be in control of their lives, rather than at the mercy of laws, agency regulations, or agency personnel (all of which can change over time). I further believe that open adoption is the hope of the future for the field of adoption.

□ □ □

I am Patricia Martinez Dorner. Rather than being a co-author of *Dear Birthmother,* I was part of the story. As an adoptive mother, I shared my early adoption experience, as well as correspondence exchanged with the birthmother of one of my daughters.

I have to admit that I did not have the typical initial fears which most adoptive parents experience. Birthparents were not a source of fright for me. However, the reason for this was not enlightenment, but, rather, total *ignorance*, as I had simply given no consideration to birthparents.

My personal involvement with adoption began with adoptive parenthood in 1978, followed by voluntarism and getting acquainted with expectant mothers in crisis who were considering adoption. These relationships impacted dramatically on me as I witnessed the multitude of emotions experienced by these young women.

When I began working in a new post-adoption program in 1980, my total immersion occurred. Now I was linked into adoption from a multitude of angles. The more I learned about the effects of closed adoption, the more I advocated openness in adoption. One of the first letters I received in my post-adoption work was from Ted, a 26-year-old adoptee seeking "assistance in solving the greatest mystery of my life." His brief words overflowed with emotion. He had reached a point in his life where he needed to risk in order to know more about his adoption. He wanted search assistance in order to contact his birthmother. As typical of many adoptees, he was not sharing this episode with his parents for fear of hurting and losing them. He was burdened with guilt and fear, yet dared to risk because of his need to know.

When I was learning about adoption issues, as a "green" prospective adoptive parent, I absorbed the two central questions of adoptees ("Who do I look like?" and "Why was I given up?") in stride. It made sense that they would wonder. What eluded me was the intensity of this need. Yet, every contact with adoptees in my post-adoption work brought the same script and the same new awareness of how driving the need is.

I located Ted's birthmother. Again, rapid lessons were learned, as this birthparent exemplified all birthparents. Her first question was "Is he alright?", followed immediately by "They told me I would forget, but I never did." I quickly learned that this was the birthparent script, as the myths regarding "not caring" and "forgetting" shattered over and over.

My children are now 8 and 10. From them, and other children, I have learned how early the issues of adoption are felt.

Vast numbers of questions about birthparents came up early in our experience. Sometimes we had answers, sometimes we did not. What mutual frustration we felt when we did not have answers—answers so readily available in today's open, fully-identified adoptions. The need to know one is loved by the absent birthfamily begins early. Confirmation of this love is vital for the emotional well being of our children.

I was involved with Kathleen Silber in the development and implementation of open adoption practice in Texas. Our practice has been revolutionary. However, only through risk-taking can progress take place. We who form the adoption triangle must learn to understand our own needs and those of the other triad members. In this manner, we will better respond to our own needs, as well as the needs of those with whom we are so inextricably interconnected.

□   □   □

We recognize that in the eighties a significant shift occurred nationwide, from agency adoption to independent adoption. There are numerous explanations for this:

The decrease in the availability of healthy infants for adoption.

The dramatic increase in infertility (one out of five American couples).

Long waiting lists at many agencies, in some cases 5 to 8 years.

The discovery by adoptive couples that they can generally adopt a baby more quickly through independent adoption.

Birthparents asserting themselves and demanding more control and openness in the adoption process, as offered by independent practitioners.

This shift has implications for agencies, which must dramatically change their programs to offer the desired openness, as well as to decrease the control and rigidity frequently inherent in agency practice. Other intermediaries must also begin to offer a better quality service (counseling, education, and support), rather than simply treating adoption as a "business transaction." We do not feel it is productive to enter into a debate between independent and agency adoption. Instead, we encourage all adoption practitioners, for the benefit of their clients, to offer the sound professional services that will be discussed in this book. Additionally, we urge birthparents and adoptive parents to educate themselves so as to better avail themselves of comprehensive and responsive services.

We will not elaborate on the myths and realities which led to the practice of open adoption and which are detailed in *Dear Birthmother*. In order to better understand the theoretical basis for this practice, we refer the reader to *Dear Birthmother*. This book will, instead, focus on the long-term impact of open adoption, sharing with the reader actual letters and case histories of individuals involved. These beautiful letters and stories will let you experience firsthand the drama of open adoption. We hope that with this book, we will continue to erode the mythology and to convey the power of open adoption in the human relationships created by the adoption process.

I know we've only just met
But feelings of love do exist,
For circumstances of
    future and past
Have given opportunities that our
    lives may share—
And though our paths may vary,
    We have a common goal
For a child to grow happy
    and healthy and wise—
In a home
    that I have chosen.

D. L. Click
Birthmother

from *Dear Birthmother* by Kathleen Silber and Phylis Speedlin, Corona Publishing Co., San Antonio, Texas, 1983

☐ 1 ☐

OPEN ADOPTION: DEFINITION, EVOLUTION, BENEFITS

Open adoption is still a relatively new and shocking concept. It shatters the myths which have traditionally surrounded the practice of adoption. Probably the most prevalent myth (surely one which all of us have believed at some point), which was identified in *Dear Birthmother*, is that "secrecy in every phase of the adoption process is necessary to protect all parties." It is important to remember that secrecy was created in a different era, when there was a tremendous stigma to a child being born out of wedlock. Secrecy was designed to protect everyone from the knowledge of "illegitimacy." However, what was designed to protect has presented many problems for all concerned, especially the adopted individual.

Even though the adopted child may feel secure and happy in his adoptive home, he still has a very natural curiosity about his roots. The adopted individual lives with a multitude of questions. The two most consistent ones are "Who do I look like?" and "Why was I given up?" The secrecy inherent in traditional adoption practice provides no answers to these questions. What results is endless wondering with no available answers. Many adopted children become troubled (yes, some even become emotionally disturbed) as they try to cope with these unknowns.

Open adoption was designed to provide answers and to eliminate the myths and misunderstandings in adoption. Open adoption is also a concept in keeping with changes in society which require honesty and openness in human relationships. Adoption involves very complex emotions and, therefore, demands the same openness that we expect in other relationships. In addition, we can no longer deny the pitfalls of traditional adoption. Instead, we must recognize that adoption is a lifelong process—it doesn't end on placement day, it is then just beginning. In their article "Open Adoption As Standard Practice," Reuben Pannor and Annette Baran state that "the secrecy, anonymity, and mystique surrounding the traditional adoptions of the past have left behind numerous psychological problems for adoptees, birthparents, and adoptive parents. This practice should not be perpetuated but must be replaced by a form of adoption that practices openness and honesty, and thereby permits a healthier and psychologically sounder adoption practice." They further state that "all adoptions, including the placement of newborn infants, should now be open, in the best interests of the child, the birthparents, and the adoptive parents."

Open Adoption and Blended Families

It is acknowledged that in our society a large proportion of families are blended families. This has been brought about by the incidence of divorce and remarriage. Thus, there are families which describe themselves as "his, hers, and ours." Children of blended families have mom and dad, stepmom and stepdad, full siblings, stepsiblings, half siblings, grandparents, stepgrandparents, and so on.

Our society strives to understand the issues that confront these families, acknowledging that there are complexities. No one would ever dream of prescribing a break in contact because divorce/remarriage occurred. We realize the reality is that sometimes the adults involved choose not to have contact for reasons beyond the scope of this book. However, society's position consistently stands in favor of contact.

There are complexities to deal with for all members in the blended family. Open adoption results in being very much like the blended family—a life journey with complexities which must be navigated with sensitivity and cooperation on the part of all those involved. When the children are of minority age, the outcomes are in the hands of the adults in their lives. The adults will chart the course.

A New Definition

In *Dear Birthmother* open adoption is defined as "any form of communication between birthparents and adoptive parents, either directly or through an intermediary." While that definition fit this practice in the early eighties, it no longer reflects what open adoption has come to represent today. As the practice has evolved, so has its definition. Open adoption advocates feel that it is essential to be clear about what constitutes open adoption. As a result, it is important to distinguish it from openness in adoption:

> Openness in adoption (or semi-open adoption) refers to various forms of communication between birthparents and adoptive parents, such as exchanging letters and pictures, meeting on a first name only basis, meeting once but not engaging in ongoing contact, etc.

> **Open adoption includes the birthparents and adoptive parents meeting one another, sharing full identifying information, and having access to ongoing contact over the years** (all three components must occur to fit this definition).* The form of ongoing contact (letters or visitation) and the frequency are determined by the individuals involved in each particular case.

Beyond a New Definition—
A New Understanding of the Relationship

In addition to our new definition of open adoption, it becomes necessary to add a new definition of the relationship between the adoptive family and the birthfamily:

> *In open adoption, the birthfamily is extended family, like other relatives within the adoptive family.*

---

* This is an excerpt from the definition which was presented by adoption experts at the Second Open Adoption Conference in Traverse City, Michigan, and which was unanimously acclaimed by those in attendance.

Our new definition recognizes the birthparents as *relatives* of the child, acknowledging that they are, in fact, related to the child. If one accepts the fact that the birthparents are relatives, then it becomes very natural to incorporate them into the child's life over the years. Acceptance of this reality is an important prerequisite to open adoption and an ongoing family relationship.

Evolving Openness

Throughout this book we will be describing adoptions which fit the new definition of open adoption, but we will also be discussing openness in adoption and closed adoptions which have been opened up. While we advocate open adoption, we do not want to negate the experiences of those not fully meeting this new definition, realizing that no adoption is static and that there is always the possibility for continued evolution of a relationship. In fact, some individuals who do not initially feel comfortable with sharing full identifying information, later do so, once they feel comfortable and "safe."

In the case of one such relationship, Ann was 36 years old and unmarried when she discovered she was pregnant. The birthfather was married to someone else, so marriage was not a realistic option at the time. Ann wanted her baby to be raised in a two-parent family, so that led her to consider adoption. After considerable thought and counseling, Ann decided to place her baby for adoption. She chose to select the adoptive parents, to meet them in person, and to have ongoing contact over the years. Ann shares her innermost feelings in the following open letter which was written a few months after placement:

> Being a private person, it's a difficult task to commit to writing my feelings of grief concerning John's adoption—especially to faceless strangers. But my determination to make as many people as possible aware of the open adoption concept makes this an easier task.
>
> No matter how much I wanted to keep my baby and be the parent in his life, I knew that I was not being fair to this little person growing inside me. I wanted him to

have more in his life than I could provide for him—yes, material things—but more importantly, the love of two parents—a family—something I was not able to give him at this time.

Being childless, thirty-six and unmarried at the time John was born, I felt certain he would be the only baby I would ever give birth to, and this made the decision to place him for adoption even harder. I remember seeing my baby's head pushing so hard to leave my body—knowing that his leaving my body meant he was also leaving me—and that this was *my choice*. I touched his little hands, arms, legs, head, body—just minutes after he was born— feeling so elated that he was healthy and whole—and thankful that I had given him life—and knowing that this too had been *my choice*.

I knew that I had to see this baby that I had carried everywhere with me for nine months—that I had to know what he looked like, what he felt like, noises he might make. How can I make someone who has never been there realize I knew that seeing John would make leaving him easier—not harder. Not seeing him would have been like denying he existed—but knowing deep down he did.

I can remember the first time I saw John in my room—feeling so overwrought with emotions. How could I leave this little person that I already loved so dearly? He seemed so oblivious to my tears each time I held him—so trusting of the support of my arms. Would he one day trust my decision concerning his adoption? Would he understand I did what I thought was best for him? Would he ever understand how much I love him? Would his parents love him as much as I do?

There seemed to be no joy in my life during those days—knowing that I would soon have to leave my baby. Where would I find the strength? How could I ever survive this separation?

It's difficult to put into words the feelings of loss, emptiness, and aloneness I felt that Thursday when I left

John at the hospital. It was a sadness I had never felt in my life.

I went back to work just over a week after John was born. I thought maybe if I was around people all day, I would stop crying all the time. And maybe if I worked all day, I could sleep at night. I wondered if I would ever feel an emotion other than sadness.

One month to the day after John's birth, I went to the agency for his placement. I would see John for the first time since that day I left him at the hospital—his one month birthday! The day his life would really begin—with his new Mommy and Daddy. I had time alone with John that afternoon—to feed him, burp him, talk to him, tell him we'd both be okay—to try to tell him why I felt I had to do this—maybe my only chance to explain to him face-to-face.

And then the time came to meet Kay and Ben—John's new parents—parents I had chosen. Had I made a good choice? Would I like them? Would they like me? Would we have anything to talk about? I was scared.

But I *did* like them—and they liked me—and we had so much to talk about. And we cried—their tears mostly tears of joy, I'm sure—an end to their struggle to have a baby. But my tears were *not* just tears of sadness that day. I felt peace, joy, relief—yes, I did feel sad. But John had a Mommy and Daddy—two people I *knew* would love him as much as I did—the two people who would raise my baby and provide for him when I could not. Two of the most special people in my life.

I *was* sad the day I left John with Kay and Ben—but it was not like the sadness I felt the day I left him at the hospital. His life was beginning—the life I had given him.

I still grieve for John some days. But if anyone had told me when I was pregnant—or even just after John was born—that I would ever experience the feelings of joy, pleasure, or pride that now outweigh the feelings of sadness, I would not have believed him. I will *always* be John's birthmother—and nothing will *ever* change that.

At the time Ann wrote this letter, Kay and Ben planned to keep in touch via letters. They had not shared full identifying information, and they did not anticipate meeting again in person. However, within a few months after placement, Kay and Ben decided they wanted to see Ann again, as they were eager to share John's growth and development with her. Their relationship quickly evolved to a fully identified and very open one. At the initiation of Kay and Ben, Ann visits in their home periodically. The adults involved have become close friends. John refers to Ann by her first name and has been told that she is his birthmother. Her relationship with him is like that of a relative. All parties perceive and validate Kay and Ben as the parents. The adults have discussed it and agree that if John ever becomes confused by Ann's presence in his life, then they will stop having face-to-face meetings for a while. They are committed to working together for whatever is best for John. Here is Kay's account of their relationship three years after placement:

> Today marks the third anniversary of the placement of our son, John, and our first meeting with his birthmother, Ann. How excited and elated we were when the call came saying the waiting was over and we could come pick up our son. We were also asked if we were still interested in meeting the birthmother. Nothing had changed—of course, we still wanted to meet her.
>
> The next two days were a whirlwind of preparation. We wanted everything to be ready for our son's homecoming. The night before we were to pick him up, we talked. We talked about the completeness our life would have with the child, the changes that would take place, and then it hit us. We were going to be meeting the birthmother of our child. It was suddenly a terrifying prospect. For the first time we realized how much we wanted *her* to like us and be happy about *her* choice for John.
>
> At the agency, we were introduced to Ann. The first few moments were a little awkward, but just the first few. The conversation was suddenly flowing and nobody felt uncomfortable. We had so much in common. There was

no need to have worried. Although it was a very emotional meeting, all of us came away from it feeling our choice was a good one. She was comfortable with us as John's parents, and we were comfortable with our decision to meet and talk with her.

The next few months were busy with the adjustments of a new baby. We exchanged letters with Ann through the agency. Somehow the relationship didn't seem complete. She had shared with us the information of her employment, so I called and we arranged to meet for lunch. The four of us had a great time.

Our friendship has been slowly cultivated and has become cherished. Ann's been to our home several times and vice versa. We were even able to arrange for her to come to our house and have Christmas Day together. There isn't a single topic that we feel uncomfortable discussing. John is starting to learn about adoption. He told me tonight that I came out of Grandma's tummy and he had come out of Ann's. Ann and I have talked about John being most important in this relationship. If he should ever become confused, we may have to temporarily shelve our friendship. To this day everything is comfortable and there are no regrets. I'm convinced that open adoption was the right choice for us.

Today, six years after placement, Ann, Kay, Ben, and John continue to have a positive and loving relationship. Ann updates us regarding her feelings about her adoption decision and the adoptive family:

I am grateful everything happened the way it did. I cannot imagine my life without Kay, Ben, and John. I thank God for an agency that was staffed with people who had the courage to handle the adoption "intelligently". . . John is such a special child and is so lucky to have Kay and Ben for parents. It has been a blessing for me to be part of his life and theirs. Every time we're with them, my husband [Ann married a few years ago] tells me how fortunate we all were and are.

Benefits in Open Adoption

In open adoption there are benefits for all three parties in the adoption triad. We will summarize them here in order to acquaint the reader with the benefits, but we will elaborate on them further in subsequent chapters as we explore the effects of open adoption over the years.

For the **adoptee**, open adoption provides answers to his normal questions. He does not have to be troubled or become obsessed with unanswered questions. He can get immediate answers when questions arise and can go on with other developmental tasks without getting stuck on adoption issues. In addition, there is an opportunity for ongoing and accurate data (e.g., if a medical problem arises, specific medical history information can be obtained). Open adoption proponents believe that this practice facilitates better mental health for children by encouraging communication within the family on the subject of adoption. In addition, with open communication within the family, the adoptee does not have to feel that he is being disloyal to his adoptive parents by being curious or asking questions about the birthparents. He is allowed to care about both sets of parents without feeling guilty. He also has a sense of belonging with his adoptive parents since he knows his birthparents selected them to parent him. This has tremendous implications for giving the child permission to develop bonds with his adoptive parents. Adoption professionals acknowledge that this is often a problem in closed adoption as children struggle with intimacy issues.

Birthparents who experience open adoption are much more at peace with their adoption decision and are better able to process their feelings of grief. We must recognize that there is always a grief experience for birthparents, as they grieve for the loss of the parenting role. However, since the birthparent in an open adoption has felt in control of her life and had made a plan for her child (instead of feeling that she had abandoned the child), these normal feelings of grief are better dealt with. She has selected and met the family and knows that she will have ongoing contact over the years, and this adds to her peace of mind. Her decision-making process reflects responsible behavior, which nurtures her self-concept. She can also feel positive about giving her child the gift of life. Furthermore, she does not have to live with any fears (e.g., "How do I know that they really love my baby?"). Knowing that she will have access to ongoing information about the child gives the birthparent a peace of mind too often absent in traditional adoption.

Adoptive parents typically have a lot of fears about the unknown, mysterious birthparents. Since they want a baby very much, they cannot imagine anyone "giving away" a baby. Once they bond with their baby, this unknown is even harder to deal with. They may even worry that if the birthmother were to see how beautiful the baby is, she would want him back. They worry that she might, in fact, even kidnap him.

Adoptive parents who have experienced open adoption generally report that, upon meeting the birthmother, they no longer fear her. The known reality (as in other things in our lives) dispels the fear. In addition, during the initial face-to-face meeting and over time, the birthmother generally communicates both that she is comfortable with her decision and that she would never do anything to disrupt the child's life. This gives adoptive parents a real peace of mind, and they do not visualize her as a threat. There are no fantasy images to deal with, but, instead, the reality of a real and caring person. The adoptive parents feel a genuine sense of closeness to the birthparents. Adoptive parents also report feeling very positive about having been chosen by the birthparents to parent their child. They feel that in later years it will be easier to convey adoption information positively. They will be able to explain that the birthparents took part in planning for their child's future by selecting them to be his parents.

Through open adoption (including the birthmother selecting the adoptive parents, meeting them, and actually handing them the baby) the birthmother, in effect, gives the adoptive parents permission to be parents. Bonding with the child is facilitated as a result of this permission. Furthermore, a heightened sense of entitlement to their child results. This is very important because adoption professionals agree that the sense of entitlement is essential for all adoptive parents to function well in their role as parents and for the child to feel that he belongs in the family.

Negatives

All life relationships, including adoption, embody complexities. After being involved with hundreds of open adoptions, we have found that the difficulties that arise are ones typical of interactions within extended family units. There can be minor disappointments—e.g., sometimes adoptive parents relate that they do not hear from the birthmother as frequently as they would like. There can be differences in lifestyles and values, and in these situations, respect for each other is vitally important. There can also be minor relationship problems. As with one's biological relatives, there are times when they may disagree with one another. When there is ongoing visitation, there also may be times when one feels as if he must "perform" for a relative. For example, the adoptive parents may feel they should make the house sparkle before the birthparent visits in order to make a good impression. Or, they may worry that their children will fight while the birthparent is visiting. These individuals will, therefore, have extra issues or "problems" to deal with than those families who do not choose ongoing visitation. As in other human relationships, they will have to be understanding of one another and work to make their relationship a positive one. The success of open adoption depends on the respectful interaction of the individuals involved.

One criticism of open adoption is that there is not enough data to know the long-term effects on the child. However, the problems associated with traditional adoption have been well documented. We must recognize that there is no "perfect adoption," just as there are no perfect biological families.

A Personal Experience with Both Concepts

Susan Dangerfield is an adoptive mother who has experienced both the traditional and the open adoption concepts. She has given us the following comparative description of the two methods.

I have so many feelings to share, I don't know where to begin. Yes I do— simply, "The truth shall set you free" and it has!

Our son Andrew was a closed adoption and Christopher was open, and there is a world of difference. With Andrew we were scared "she" was going to try to take him back. With Christopher, we met his birthmother, Susan, the day of placement and had a chance to talk (I should say cry and be nervous a lot) before the placement. I'll never forget as Susan and her mother were getting ready to go—we all hugged each other tightly and they both said "We feel so much better now that we've met you." On that note we started tearing up again.

I can't tell you how much better Steve and I felt about going to meet our new son. Since we had met Susan and knew first hand her reasons for choosing adoption, we felt more secure, and I know she felt better and more content after meeting us. We weren't some nameless, faceless couple who would be raising her child. We were Steve and Susan—two people who loved her very much and she knew it, and that love was being returned to us. By simply being honest and open, a very rough time for both parties was turned into a very warm situation. I know it was a very hard day for Susan but our meeting made it a little more bearable. We as adoptive parents had to come face-to-face with feelings we hadn't experienced the first time, like seeing Susan's pain and crying with her and knowing that when she left it would be without Chris. Those were not pleasant things to have to deal with but I'm glad we did. It made us much more aware and sensitive to how birthmothers feel.

Susan and I stay in touch usually by letters. There is no pressure for either of us to write—therefore we write when we want to and not because we have to. It's such a neat surprise when her letters come and after reading them, they are carefully tucked away for Chris.

We have since met Andy's birthmother, Karen, and she is an absolute love too. We stay in touch more by phone and when she calls even after a long period we pick up like old friends and yak our heads off. She tells me about what she's up to and I do the same. It is so warm and loving! The part I regret, and still have a hard time dealing with, is that Karen went two solid years without knowing anything about Andy. She didn't know if he was dead or alive (she could only wonder), that he was the apple of our eye, and that his smile covers his entire face. The sad thing is that none of it had to be that way. Many adoptive parents like myself wanted to believe the myth that "she will forget" over time. It's much easier that way. But the fact is, she loves this child too and can never forget. We must always remember that "a birthmother relinquishes her parental rights—certainly not her feelings."

The genuine love between Susan, Karen and ourselves was definitely nurtured by the fact that we all respect each other tremendously. There was also an excellent counseling and educational process that helped make the base of our triangle strong.

Finally, I would never say open adoption is the only way—certainly there is always a case that is an exception. Though just as society is changing and becoming more open and honest, adoption too needs to undergo those same changes. All our lives, we've been taught to be honest! Then why now are we keeping secrets? We all know a secret doesn't ever stay a secret! With open adoption, there are no secrets!

Indeed—the truth shall set you free!

□ 2 □

ESSENTIAL INGREDIENTS IN OPEN ADOPTION

There are several key prerequisites and ingredients of a successful open adoption:

Myth-Free Adoption

Before one can accept and embrace open adoption, it is important to work through the normal feelings of fear and threat that are evoked when one is first introduced to the concept of open adoption. These feelings of threat are particularly characteristic of prospective adoptive parents. Once a couple has gone through years of wanting a baby (and countless fertility tests and/or treatments) it is very typical to want to "own" the adopted child and to not want to think about another set of parents in the child's life. There is a desire to "make this their biological child" and forget about the adoption experience. Birthparents initially may also be fearful of open adoption, thinking that it might be easier to go on with their lives pretending that the pregnancy and adoption never occurred. While these may be very typical initial reactions, it is essential to move past them and take an in-depth look at adoption myths, issues, and realities.

We must recognize that stereotypes and myths influenced and dominated traditional adoption practice, as well as the way each of us view, or has viewed, adoption. *Dear Birthmother* identified and dispelled some of the most significant myths, such as the secrecy myth discussed in the last chapter. Each individual must assess his own attitudes and stereotypes and be able to move past the myths. Myth-free thinking acknowledges that the birthparents love (and will always love) the child they are placing for adoption, that secrecy is not conducive to healthy adoptive functioning, and that it is normal for an adoptee to be curious about his identity and roots. The latter is not a rejection of the adoptive parents. By dispelling the myths, the individual will discover that his initial feelings of fear and threat disappear.

From Myths to Realities

Having acknowledged the myths, we must move on to realities, as well as a new definition of adoption. One reality is that adoption is a lifelong experience. Another reality is (no matter how much the adoptive couple may wish that this were a child born to them) that the adoptee will always have two sets of parents. When adoptive parents accept this important reality, they can truly accept adoption as it is, rather than how they might wish it were. In addition, they can embrace open adoption because they can acknowledge (rather than be threatened by) the birthparents' role in the child's life. In fact, they will *want* contact with the birthparents because they will realize its importance to the child. This reflects back to the definition of adoption in *Dear Birthmother*:

> *Adoption is the process of accepting the*
> *responsibility of raising an individual*
> *who has two sets of parents.*

Resolution of Grief

Grief accompanies both the infertility experience and the birthparent experience. In the past, adoption was not viewed in connection with grief or loss. However, adoption professionals have increasingly become aware of the part which grief and resolution of grief play in the adoption experience.

Birthparents

It is perhaps easier to understand grief in relation to birthparents since they, in effect, lose a child. However, society has traditionally been insensitive to the birthparents' loss, probably because it was believed they voluntarily chose to place the child for adoption. Furthermore, in the past, out of wedlock pregnancies were viewed as shameful, which resulted in these situations being handled with secrecy. Birthparents were often sent away from home to have the baby so no one would know about the pregnancy. Prior to delivery, they were "knocked out" so they would not remember giving birth, and they returned home to "forget." Grief was not expected; therefore, they were not prepared for it. Not even helping professionals had any awareness that these emotions would surface. In reality, birthparents did grieve but received no support or validation for the normalcy of their grief.

Today helping professionals recognize that *all* birthparents grieve for their children and they will never forget the children. Even though they choose adoption (including open adoption), they still experience a loss—the loss of the parenting role and all it entails. And they grieve for this loss. They experience all of the stages of grief (shock, denial, anger, depression, and acceptance) just as if someone had died. Counseling helps them prepare for the grief experience while they are still pregnant and cope with it after placement. A birthparent support group can be especially helpful during the grieving process.

It has been consistently observed that open adoption enables birthparents to work through the normal feelings of grief much more successfully. However, it is important to add that grief is not a one time event. Feelings of loss and grief resurface at various intervals in one's life, and birthparents should be prepared for this.

Adoptive Parents

We typically view adoptive parents as full of happiness and joy when adopting a baby. We do not usually relate grief to their adoption experience. However, in order to be effective adoptive parents and to accept adoption realities and issues, adoptive parents must first come to terms with infertility. Infertility is a grief experience, although traditionally it has not been viewed as such. Infertility is a loss—it is a loss of the imaginary or fantasy child (the child the couple imagines would have been born to them). They will go through all of the normal stages of grieving for this loss, just as if they had lost a child through death. However, society does not relate to or understand the loss in infertility because as Patricia Irwin Johnston indicates in *An Adoptor's Advocate*, the loss is invisible.

An Adoptor's Advocate also identifies some of the losses in infertility. We believe that the most significant of these is the loss of control. Infertile couples experience a loss of control in the bedroom (where they cannot accomplish what every other couple seems able to achieve), in dealing with the medical profession, in dealing with the adoption intermediary, and, finally, in dealing with the birthmother (because she holds the power to decide who will parent her baby). These factors combine to make the loss of control a very significant one and one which infertile couples must come to terms with before adopting.

When a couple is experiencing infertility, doctors and others often suggest adoption as the magic "pill" which will take care of the pain of infertility. As a result, some couples rush to adopt before dealing with their grief. If a couple adopts before they have worked through the stages of grief (e.g., while they are still depressed), the pain can actually become more intense. Every time they look at their adopted baby, he can be a constant reminder of their infertility, resulting in increased depression. So it is important for infertile couples to get counseling or take the necessary time (time is an important healer) to work through their feelings of grief *before* adopting; otherwise, the adopted child will always be "second best." He cannot compete with the fantasy child, who is always perfect. Support groups, such as Resolve (national infertility support group), can also be helpful.

We implore prospective adoptive parents to be honest with themselves. If infertility is still a source of anguish or distress, do not adopt! We are often asked, "How do I know when my feelings about infertility are resolved?" We have found that the experience is similar to being in love. When one is in love, one *knows*. So it is with infertility. The turning point resulting in acceptance and peacefulness can best be identified by the individual himself.

It is important to add that if the infertility issue is not resolved prior to adoption, it can impact the parent-child relationship over the years. One of the first direct confrontations with infertility comes when the child asks if he grew in mommy's womb. At this point old feelings may surface, and it may be difficult for the mother to discuss birth with her child since she could not accomplish a pregnancy and birth herself. Infertility issues may surface at other times, as well. Many adult adoptees have shared with us the fact that they realized their parents still had problems with infertility, which were manifested in different ways over the years. For example, many adopted women have told us that when they were having a baby themselves, their adoptive mothers could not come to the hospital to visit them; it was too painful for them to see their daughters do something they could not do—give birth. This signifies how powerful unresolved infertility can be, even twenty or thirty years later.

So we have become increasingly aware of the power of the pain of infertility and the critical need for couples to deal with the pain and go through the necessary stages of grieving before adoption. Adoption professionals must also understand the loss and grief issues in adoption and help their clients recognize and deal with these issues. However, it is also essential to recognize that even if infertility is resolved, it doesn't go away. As Patricia Irwin Johnston states "As with any wound, it heals with a scar which can be reopened again at an unexpected time. Infertility's scars remain on the soul long after the wounds have healed." And, as Barbara Eck Menning notes in her book *Infertility: A Guide For The Childless Couple*: "My infertility resides in my heart as an old friend. I do not hear from it for weeks at a time, and then, a moment, a thought, a baby announcement or some such thing, and I will feel the tug—maybe even be sad or shed a few tears. And I think 'There's my old friend.' It will always be part of me . . . "

The poem* below, from *An Adoptor's Advocate* beautifully speaks to the issues of loss and resolution in infertility:

---

*The authors gratefully acknowledge permission to use this poem.

Burial

Today I closed the door of the nursery
    I have kept for you in my heart.

I can no longer stand in its doorway.
I have waited for you there so long.
I cannot forever live on the periphery
    of the dream world we share, and you
    cannot enter my world.

I have fought to bring you across the
    threshold of conception and birth.
I have fought time, doctors, devils, and
    God Almighty.
I am weary and there is no victory.

Other children may someday live in my
    heart but never in your place.

I can never hold you. I can never really
    let you go. But I must go on.
The unborn are forever trapped within the
    living but it is unseemly for the
    living to be trapped forever by the
    unborn.

                E. Van Clef

In open adoption, resolution of infertility and resolution of the loss for birthparents are even more essential than in traditional adoption. As these individuals have contact with one another over the years, they will be confronted on an ongoing basis with the reality of each other. The adoptive parents cannot pretend this is a child born to them, and the birthparent has to recognize that someone else is parenting her child.

Counseling and Education

Counseling and education for both adoptive parents and birthparents are essential ingredients in an open adoption. Adoption agencies and other intermediaries have a responsibility to provide these for both parties so as to prepare and enable them to deal with adoption issues. They also have the responsibility to keep abreast of all the new learning that is taking place nationwide in order to better prepare their clients.

Pregnancy Counseling

Professional counseling should be provided to both the birthmother and birthfather to help them explore *all* options and to help them be sure adoption is right for them. Since adoption is a permanent plan, it is important that it be well thought out. Only then will adoption be a decision they can live with. Adoption counselors must also prepare the birthparents for the grief process while they are still pregnant, and then provide grief counseling after placement when they are going through the stages of grief. Providing reading materials pertaining to the grief experience is helpful. Sometimes birthparents believe they will be spared the pain, and, therefore, when they experience it and acknowledge it, validation through reading becomes invaluable.

Open adoption diminishes denial on the part of birthparents. Often those who refuse to participate in openness do so to avoid the pain they anticipate. Instead, they heighten and prolong the grief. Those involved with openness allow themselves to process it incrementally by confronting it. The result is a sense of well-being.

In addition, counseling services should be available to the birth grandparents (and other extended family), since they are experiencing their own crisis and pain. The birthmother's parents (particularly in the case of teenage pregnancy) experience guilt feelings regarding their daughter's pregnancy and wonder how they "failed" as parents. They may blame themselves or feel responsible for the pregnancy. They also confront their own feelings about "giving up" a grandchild, possibly their first. They may feel guilty if they do not want to parent the baby themselves or help their daughter parent the child. These are normal reactions to the crisis of a pregnancy in a family. Counseling helps the birth grandparents deal with these normal feelings and enables them to participate in the adoption plan.

It is important to include birthfathers in the adoption planning, as well as through the years. Unfortunately, many birthfathers deal with the crisis by denying paternity, taking flight, or plunging into emotional denial. The expectant mother has often already experienced the state of denial—"I'm not pregnant, my period is just late." Eventually, she must acknowledge the child's presence within her as her body grows and movement is felt. The males do not experience these realities, and, therefore, the stage of denial is often more prolonged. Furthermore, when services from the adoption professional are refused, the birthmothers often are thrust into the counseling role.

A major benefit of open adoption is that when the birthfather can face the reality of the child and his adoption, support and participation modes are available. *The emotional journey of loss experienced by birthfathers is totally parallel to that of birthmothers.* However, many males choose to hide this from others. Our society grooms males for a "macho" posture, which excludes the showing of feelings—particularly feelings of grief that often include tears. Brave is the man who allows himself to confront his own grief and reveal it to outside observers.

When a birthfather allows himself to deal with his loss, he avoids the tremendous guilt so often represented. He does not have to punish himself for the rest of his life for not "assuming responsibility" for the care and raising of his child . Emotionally healthier, he can continue to grow, rather than experience emotional stunting that affects all segments of his life.

Education

It is imperative that adoptive parents participate in an intensive educational process, which focuses on sensitizing them to adoption issues and realities. In effect, this is training for more effective adoptive parenting. This educational process is probably the single most important service that adoption professionals can provide their clients.

Over the years we have developed increasingly effective workshops which maximize the learning experience while allowing for the emotional processing of adoption issues.

We have implemented an educational process which consists of two or three sessions of three to four hours each. In addition to the group discussions, there is required reading, which reinforces the material presented in the sessions.

The workshops focus on the unique issues facing each triad member and how these interrelate. Through the use of panels of triad members, these sessions dramatically help prospective adoptive parents move from myths to realities. In our experience the most impacting is the contact with birthparents. The goal of the educational sessions is to expand the couples' mind set from the infant stage to a broader life experience model. The sessions also help the couples feel more comfortable with open adoption. By using a multi-dimensional approach, learning is maximized; each element reinforces the other.

Counseling and the First Meeting

It is essential that open adoption be offered with quality counseling services. Clients should not simply be thrown into a face-to-face meeting without any preparation or support. Adoption is not a business transaction conducted by lawyers or doctors, but, rather, a complex life experience.

At the time of the face-to-face meeting, it is normal for prospective adoptive parents and birthparents to feel some anxiety. The counselor dispels much of this through preparatory and debriefing sessions. Counselors remain available over time, sharing broad base expertise with their clients.

Other Ingredients

There are other ingredients which facilitate a positive open adoption experience. Frequently observed within the most comfortable participants is a strong self-concept. Insecure people have difficulty with the reality of two sets of parents. They are threatened by it and, as a result, feel more insecure. They have a tendency to always feel inadequate compared to the birthparents (again, fertility vs. infertility). Conversely, adoptive parents with strong self-concepts are easily able to handle the realities involved; they do not feel a need to compete with the birthparents.

Flexibility in adoptive parents is also of major importance. This quality has to do with the ability to accept differences and to adapt to changing circumstances and fluctuations in emotions and relationships. As with any parents, strong parenting skills also contribute to positive and healthy family interactions. Among these skills are communication and discipline.

We believe that all of the elements in open adoption which we have discussed are actually essential to *any* adoption. However, they become more important in open adoption because of the direct and ongoing contact birthparents and adoptive parents have with one another. These ingredients facilitate a healthier relationship between the parties and a more positive adoption. We encourage prospective adoptive parents and birthparents to seek out an adoption intermediary which offers the kinds of adoption services we have discussed. In the event that the services located do not meet these criteria, knowledgeable participants are able to seek them elsewhere. Since adoption is a lifelong process, the participants deserve comprehensive services, and they should not settle for less.

The following case history describes the relationship between one birthmother and adoptive couple who experienced all of the issues which we have discussed:

Becky, pregnant and unmarried at age 21, did not consider abortion. She planned to parent her baby, as she already knew that she loved her baby very much. However, later in the pregnancy she decided that adoption was the best plan because she wanted a two-parent, stable family situation for her baby. She also wanted a mother who would be able to stay home with the baby. If she chose to parent the baby herself, she would have to work in order to support herself and the baby. Therefore, she would not able to be a full-time parent.

Counseling helped Becky look at the issues and make a decision she could live with. She came to have a realistic view of both single parenthood and adoption. It was painful and difficult for her to place her baby, Sarah, for adoption; yet she felt strongly that she was making the right decision.

Becky also chose open adoption. In fact, she commented that she did not think she would have been able to place Sarah for adoption if open adoption had not been an option. Becky chose an adoptive couple who were open to ongoing visitation. She relates "With open adoption, I will be able to know how the baby is doing. I will know she is okay and in a good home. I gave her up out of love, and it makes me happy to know she is okay." Becky and the adoptive parents, Robert and Sandra, keep in touch through letters, phone calls, and visits a couple of times a year. When asked how much contact she would like, Becky replied "Just as much as they will let me have." Becky is open to whatever contact Robert and Sandra initiate. She states that she will also understand if at some point they want to reduce the contact if it ever becomes confusing to Sarah.

Robert and Sandra acknowledge that they had all of the typical fears of birthparents before going through the educational sessions which their adoption intermediary offered. Now, "We don't have those fears anymore. We know that Becky loves Sarah and wouldn't do anything to disrupt Sarah's life. That's the plus for open adoption."

Robert and Sandra feel very comfortable with having Becky visit in their home. Sandra notes, "Sarah will have a very special relationship with Becky— kind of like a distant relative. She will grow to love Becky and will understand that she was given up in love. But it won't be shared parenting— we'll always be the parents." Sandra further elaborates, "Becky is a part of our family because she's a part of Sarah's family—and Sarah's a part of us— Becky is like an extended family member, and we love her." Sandra also feels that the openness which they are experiencing will benefit Sarah. "Because we have answers for Sarah's questions, there will be a feeling of continuity of identity for her."

When Becky was asked what she would do if Sarah ran away from home as a teenager and appeared on her doorstep, she replied "I would say 'No, Sandra is your mother,' and I would take her back home." Becky feels good about her decision and about open adoption, noting "I love them all, and I know Sarah is happy." Robert and Sandra feel very confident about the future.

□ 3 □

THE INFANT

Obviously with an infant, the child is not an equal participant in the relationship between his birthparents and adoptive parents. However, the initial relationship between the adults involved plants the seed for a relationship which will ultimately include the child as the central participant. First, the adults must build a relationship based on trust, as well as respect of each other's roles.

The Honeymoon

Usually there is a "honeymoon" period, where the birthparents will deny any pain and will be convinced that they picked "the best adoptive parents in the whole world," and where the adoptive parents will think they have the most wonderful baby in the world and the ideal birthmother. During this honeymoon period, it is important for the adoptive parents to have some "space." That is, they need time (without interference by the birthmother) to bond with the baby and establish their own intimate relationship as a family. If there is too frequent contact with the birthmother during these first few weeks, the couple can over-identify with her and her pain, thereby continuing to view the baby as "her baby." We are not suggesting that there should be no contact between the adults involved during the honeymoon period (in fact, contact during this time can be beneficial to both parties); we are simply pointing out some of the risks of extremely frequent contact. In practice, most birthparents are very sensitive to the family's need to bond and are not overly intrusive during this time period.

In fact, some birthparents prefer to have more limited contact during the honeymoon period and beyond (sometimes up to a year or two) because this is a very emotional time for them (remember they are going through the stages of grief). They may find that seeing the baby in person or frequent other contact is too painful. They may need time to heal the wounds and to be able to see the baby without becoming overly emotional (usually they do not want the adoptive parents to think of them as a "basket case"). Although the length of time needed and the effects of contact will vary in each case, one must be sensitive to the right of birthparents to have whatever "space" is needed.

Conversely, some birthparents have a tendency to become overly close to the adoptive parents, as the result of the close relationship they shared during the pregnancy/birth. In fact, the shared birth experience (in cases where the adoptive parents are in the delivery room) creates a real sense of intimacy. Sometimes an outgrowth of this closeness is that when the birthmother is going through the normal grieving, she turns to the adoptive parents as her counselors. It is only natural that she would turn to someone she feels close to discuss and share her pain. However, when this happens, the adoptive parents are generally overwhelmed and unable to deal with the grief and feelings expressed (e.g., "Sometimes I feel like I made a mistake and should have kept my baby") at a time when they are bonding with their baby. They naturally cannot handle these feelings and often misinterpret them (they may forget that the birthmother is going through the normal stages of grief). Therefore, it is extremely important that the birthmother turn to her adoption counselor for counseling, not the adoptive parents. The trained adoption professional is also better able to help the birthmother work through her feelings of grief.

There is another negative outcome which can occur from the closeness which the birthmother and adoptive parents experience, especially in situations where they have shared the very intimate and emotional experience of being in the delivery room together, or when a very close and intimate relationship develops over time. We must recognize that the close relationship which may evolve in open adoption is not clearly defined in our society—i.e., the birthmother is not a relative in the traditional sense, but she is more than a friend—it has to do with intimacy. As the relationship becomes intimate, there may be an emotional component which could be scary. Emotions may be felt which have sexual overtones. If this occurs, it tends to be confusing and distressing for those involved. However, it is understandable that a sense of closeness, caring, and love occurs (this is normal). In fact, most open adoption relationships become very intimate and intense. The adoptive parents and birthparents become bonded to one another as a result of the relationship which they all share with the child. Insight, sensitivity, and understanding are important ingredients in preserving a healthy relationship. The adoptive parents and birthmother must be committed to the adoption and the ongoing interaction which they will all have over the years, as well as determined not to jeopardize it.

Bonding and Entitlement

As mentioned previously, through open adoption the birthmother, in effect, gives the adoptive couple permission to be parents. This (particularly the birthmother physically handing the baby to the family) is very powerful, and it is something which is absent in traditional adoption. The physical transfer of the baby from the birthparents to the adoptive parents is a very important ritual. In other aspects of life, ceremonies, rituals, or rites of passage are very important as one moves from one stage to another, and this applies to adoption, as well. The actual placement or placement ceremony, similar to a marriage ceremony, is an important ritual in the adoption process. It facilitates the grieving process for the birthparents.

In addition, the adoptive parents witness and participate in the birthmother's grief. By witnessing her emotions, the adoptive parents internalize the feelings and do not forget them. This enables them to acknowledge the very real loss of the birthparents, rather than to block or deny it. The intimacy of the placement itself breeds closeness, as shared pain is bonding. Those who allow themselves to feel the birthmother's pain have heightened sensitivity and are more in touch with their own feelings (and the child's feelings in later years). Of course, the adoptive parents must balance this with their joy at becoming parents. One does not ordinarily experience such extreme happiness and sadness at the same time, which makes open adoption truly unique. In addition, the birthparents, who are going through their own grief and loss, have the opportunity to participate in the adoptive couple's joy. In spite of their pain, most birthmothers say, "I'll never forget the look in their eyes when they first saw my baby." This participation in the family's happiness helps them feel more at peace with their decision.

The shared ritual of placement also gives the adoptive parents permission to parent. Adoptive parents usually report very quick bonding as the result of this permission. In fact, we have consistently witnessed quicker bonding for families with open adoption than those with traditional or semi-open adoptions. Instead of unknowns, fears, or feelings of threat, the family with open adoption experiences knowns, realities, and positives, all of which facilitate bonding with the infant (conversely, the fear of losing the child to the birthmother inhibits bonding).

One adoptive mother, Alberta Taubert, comments on her personal experience with bonding:

> Jim and I believe the bonding was quicker having met Christy. Christy essentially gave us "permission" to parent Jordan. When we first met, Christy told us why she had chosen adoption for her daughter, why she had selected us as the adoptive parents, and so much more. I know that the meeting was *so* much more powerful and meaningful for us than had we just been given the information on paper. The most dramatic part of our meeting came when Christy left the room, came back with Jordan in her arms (4 days old), walked up to us and placing her in my arms said, "Here, Mom."

Another adoptive mother, Laurie Morkert, compares her experience of bonding through traditional adoption and open adoption:

With Daniel (open adoption), we felt the bonding was *much* quicker due to the openness and due to the fact that he was placed with us at 3 days of age, as opposed to the mandatory *5-week* wait with Cara (Tennessee law). . . .

I truly felt (even though we were thrilled with our baby girl) that there was a "vacuum" present on Cara's adoption day. After I learned about open adoption, I knew that vacuum was that Cara's birthmother was absent that day. . . . This experience was so different from our experience with Daniel. We were thrilled to meet his birthmother and her mother and brother. Meeting her only intensified our bonding with Daniel, and subsequent meetings with her only served to reinforce our feelings of closeness to Daniel and to her.

Missy Mial shares her experience with bonding:

I remember feeling so good about having met Sherry (birthmother). Her determination and confidence regarding her adoption decision really made it easy for me to bond with John Paul. It was as if I had been given permission (or, rather, approval) to indulge in this wonderful feeling that was taking place. I know I couldn't have relaxed and allowed the bonding to take place as quickly and strongly if I had been worrying about his birthmother. How is she? Is she okay? Is she heartbroken ? Did she really want to do this? I would have driven myself crazy with worry. As it was—I felt a lot of pain and heartbreak for her—it was clear she loved this baby. But she demonstrated to us her happiness at having chosen us to be his parents, and it made the sadness I felt easier to live with.

Even with quick bonding, adoptive parents frequently experience occasional feelings of sadness (as Missy describes above) during the early weeks as they identify with the birthmother's pain. Actually, it is vitally important that adoptive parents be aware of and remember the birthmother's pain. This empathy and reality are positives for adoptive parents to experience, as this will enable them to be more sensitive and empathic in discussing adoption with the child in later years. Alberta Taubert describes her experience with grief:

> Meeting Christy not only gave us permission to parent, it also made us vividly aware of the pain caused by her decision and the love for her child. I remember those first few weeks, late at night when I would be feeding Jordan, I felt so happy and so fulfilled, yet I would begin to cry because at the same time I felt so sad. I soon realized and understood, because of our counseling, that I was crying for Christy, I felt her loss, I felt her pain.

Another result of open adoption is that the adoptive parents feel a real sense of entitlement to their child. The permission to parent and quick bonding noted above contribute to this sense of entitlement. In effect, the birthmother *gives* the adoptive parents entitlement to the child because, in spite of her grief, she *wants* them to parent the child. As Lois Melina notes in *Raising Adopted Children*, "Developing a sense that a child 'belongs' in the family, even though she wasn't born into it, is a crucial task for adoptive parents. Unless adoptive parents develop a sense that the child is really theirs, they will have difficulty accepting their right to act as parents." So, it is significant that open adoption facilitates a sense of entitlement.

Judy Albrecht comments on bonding and entitlement:

> I love *all* of my child. Nothing is denied to her or *about* her. My bond is, I feel, far more powerful as a result. Open adoption increased my sense of entitlement and helped me realize the greater creativity involved in parenting, not birthing.

The following case demonstrates an adoptive mother who experienced the sense of permission to parent and feelings of entitlement and a birthmother who is at peace with her decision.

> Kate was 16 and a high school student when she became pregnant. Her parents were not supportive of her parenting the baby as a single parent. Marriage was not a

realistic option. Kate also wanted to finish high school and go on to college. So she turned to adoption. While she was still pregnant, Kate noted, "People think it's so easy to give up a baby, and they think if you really loved the baby you wouldn't give her up. I can't imagine giving up this baby and never thinking of her again—that's ridiculous." Counseling helped Kate deal with her decision and with the normal grief afterward.

Today (several years later), Kate still has contact with her child, Amy, and the adoptive parents who she selected and met. Kate notes, "When I see her I don't want her back. I would never go steal her away because I know where she is. It's a good feeling to see them and know she's okay." It is important for birthparents to realize that even with open adoption there is still a grief process. Kate notes, "There's a lot of pain. But getting letters and pictures— and seeing her in person really helps. I know she's loved and well taken care of. I wouldn't be okay today if not for open adoption—I would have probably been crazy by now if I didn't know she was okay."

Amy's adoptive mother, Jan, notes, "I have permission to parent now through knowing Kate." She does not think she would feel that sense of "permission" without open adoption. She adds, "We feel very safe with her." Kate further states "I chose adoption more for Amy than for myself. She is a beautiful little girl, and I don't regret it. I wish I hadn't gotten pregnant at age 16, but I don't regret my decision. I feel a lot better about myself than I would have if I had had an abortion. I know Amy is healthy and happy, and I know I made the adoptive parents very happy. I love them all."

Jan knows that Amy will have a "deep need to know about Kate." They feel they have enough information to satisfy her curiosity. However, they recognize that Amy might at a time of rebellion want to run to Kate. "We will all work it out together. We three adults may have to say someday 'No, you can't go back. This is your home.' We will be together in supporting each other and recognizing each others roles. From the first day we met Kate she referred to me as the Mother and my husband as the Daddy. The openness has eliminated our fears. Before we adopted we had the typical fears that the birthmother was going to want the baby back or that the child might run away to search for the birthmother. As we got into it, we realized that the birthmother was no longer a threat. The only thing you fear is fear itself. We are dealing with realities, and they are good realities. We have a very upbeat relationship with Kate. We feel at peace with ourselves, and we know Kate is also at peace. We wouldn't do it any other way."

The Evolution of the Relationship

The relationship between the adoptive parents and birthparents is an ever-evolving one. It is important that there be room in any agreement (especially if it is a written agreement) for the individuals to grow and change. No relationship is static, and people and their needs may change over the years. An open adoption agreement must be flexible enough to accommodate those changes. Therefore, it is preferable for a written open adoption agreement to incorporate flexibility, rather than being overly specific and restrictive. If it is not or if there is conflict, the participants should seek out adoption mediation to work through any differences and reach a compromise.

Initially (prior to meeting one another) the adoption participants reach some decision on how much openness they are comfortable with. This preliminary decision is made based on some unknowns. Once they meet and are faced with reality, they usually refine and re-define their openness agreement. After placement, grieving, and bonding, the participants may decide they want more or less contact than they had previously thought or agreed to. However, it is not fair or appropriate for adoptive couples to "agree to anything" to get a baby and then renege on the agreement afterward. They are morally obligated (and in some cases legally obligated) to whatever is in their agreement, unless the other party agrees to the changes. In other words, if the birthmother chose to place her baby with the couple on the basis of certain conditions (e.g., ongoing visitation), the couple should follow through. Changing from "more" contact to "less" is usually difficult and frequently involves mediation, whereas changing from "less" to "more" (the more common direction we see change occurring) is much easier.

Typically, after the adoptive couple has bonded with the baby, they realize cognitively and emotionally that this is "their" baby, and they feel less threatened by the birthparent. As a result, they may decide that they are comfortable with more openness than they had previously thought. Similarly, as the birthmother moves through the grief process, she realizes that she will never forget her baby and that contact helps rather than hurts. So she may also feel comfortable with increased openness. As the trust in one another and the comfort level grows, the relationship will continue to develop. It is not unusual for an adoptive couple who are engaging in ongoing visitation to think back to their initial feelings about openness and to remember that originally they would have never believed that they would have agreed to (let alone *want*) ongoing visitation. In fact, most adoptive couples (after losing their fears and integrating adoption realities) decide they are comfortable with more openness than they originally thought. Sometimes the couple wants more contact than the birthparent is comfortable with because they realize the importance of maintaining the relationship for the sake of their child.

Linda Adams recalls the evolution of their relationship with four-year-old Casey's birthmother:

> At first we went through the agency, but found that letters and pictures were taking too long to arrive. At that point (when Casey was still an infant), we felt comfortable with the family (they were like family) and exchanged every thing (full identifying information). We don't regret the decision and feel it only broadened our love for them as part of the family.

Over the years the Adams family has corresponded and sent pictures regularly to the birthmother and her parents, as well as visited in person on a regular basis.

Yvonne, adoptive mother of Ashley, age 5, recalls a similar evolution, as well as frustration with the agency being the intermediary for contact:

> We found the correspondence through the agency to be too slow. We might receive a letter mailed two months prior to the date we received it. This is when we opted to start visiting and meeting with them. The visits were initially infrequent. But as we got to know them both, we felt very comfortable with the visits. Our visits with them (both birthparents) began to be more frequent, and Ashley was no longer the main source for our meetings. We found that we had made some very good friends.

Time does not stand still for the birthparents, and they, too, go on with their lives, experiencing changes which may affect the relationship and frequency of contact. For example, marriage will add potentially new relationships. Mates who are comfortable with adoption free the birthmother to continue to process her decision emotionally and to participate in the agreed-upon contact.

Alberta Taubert shares with us how her family participated in Christy's marriage three years after placement:

> In May we were invited to Christy and Gary's wedding. Gary is a caring man who understands and is a part of our relationship.
>
> It was a beautiful wedding. I think the only wedding that has touched me as much was our own. I remember sitting there, just trying to take it all in. It was so special to be at our child's birthmother's wedding! I felt very proud, in fact, I felt like this is what it must be like to see your daughter get married. I cried for her happiness, just seeing her up there looking so beautiful. I was also proud that she had come this far. I have always had a tremendous amount of respect for Christy (for making the difficult decision not to parent Jordan) and now she was getting married and starting a new life.
>
> At the reception, Christy's parents, Pete and Susan, who have always been supportive of Christy and who

were with us on placement day, introduced us to the rest of the family. They would say, "This is Jim and Alberta, Jordan's parents," and you could just see everyone's faces light up. It was a wonderful feeling. One of Christy's uncles even commented that Jordan has Christy's beautiful curly hair—which she does.

A little while later all of the children joined the group (they had been playing in the nursery). Christy was getting ready to go and suggested that we bring Jordan into the changing room. This was really a special moment. We walked into the room and Jordan said, "You look so pretty." Christy knelt down, held Jordan's hands, and talked softly to her. I don't know what she was saying. I was busy fighting back tears, and Jim was taking pictures. It was *their* special moment. We then moved outside, and Jordan threw the first bag of rice at her birthmother and her new husband.

A Positive, Evolving Relationship— from Letters to Visits

Debbie Scannell was 26 years old when she decided to place her baby for adoption six years ago. She felt strongly about wanting to meet the adopting parents. However, there were no additional visits planned after the initial meeting; instead, she expected to stay in touch through letters and pictures. Debbie describes her adoption decision, as well as her evolution to ongoing visitation, which she has been engaging in for several years:

I chose adoption for many reasons. I had a religious background which made abortion out of the question. I thought long and hard about keeping the baby, and I really wanted it to work out so I could. But being the practical, rational person I am that option just kept coming up short. I wanted the best for my child, and at that time the best was not with me. I would be working full-time and/or going to school, leaving little time for me to parent my child. It would be left up to family, friends, and daycare. The bottom line was that I was not emotionally and financially prepared to raise a child on my own. I wanted a secure, established, prepared home with two parents for my child.

I spent the entire nine months preparing for the birth and adoption. I had chosen a wonderful family and planned to meet with them before the birth. But I went into labor the day I was to meet them and delivered a beautiful, healthy baby girl. Her birth was an absolutely wonderful experience. I was immediately in love with this child (which made the whole decision a little harder). I spent time in the nursery holding and feeding her, telling her why I was doing what I was doing, and that I loved her. It was because I loved her so much that I made the decision I did. It was a very emotional time, and I shed more tears than I thought humanly possible. The hardest part was leaving the hospital 'empty-handed.' I had taken care of this child for nine months, and now someone else was going to take her home.

A few days later I met with the adoptive parents. They were far beyond my fantasies and expectations. No questions were left in my mind that they would give to her the things I wanted her to have. More tears were shed, and we planned, at that time, to have letters and pictures for communication. They received my daughter on Christmas eve, what a wonderful Christmas present!

Her parents were wonderful about pictures and letters. I looked forward to getting these, and every time I did I felt better about my decision. I had fantasies about running into the adoptive parents someday, and about two years later it happened. I saw the mom and she was delighted to see me and asked if I would like to see my birth daughter. That first meeting was incredible. Was this the little baby I held in the hospital? She was so beautiful, happy, and content—just as I had planned from the beginning!

Since that first meeting we have been in contact frequently. I have been to their home, and they to mine on several occasions. Full sharing of names, etc., came with time—they had to know they could trust me. I have always said I would never do anything to jeopardize her happiness, and I mean it. That would make a mockery of my entire decision to let someone else raise her. Over the years a sort of disassociation occurs in that I know I gave birth to her and I love her, but she is not my child. She belongs to someone else, and it's OK. Even when she gives me a big hug, which makes me feel very good knowing she is affectionate toward me, I still feel good (if not better) about everything. I'm proud of her and my decision, and every time I see her it's a little more reinforced. Future visits are still unsettled. So far everything has gone great, but it really depends on how she deals with it emotionally as she grows. I trust her parents' judgment and their proven openness with me. . . .

A Relationship Which Encountered Problems

David and Pam Jensen met their child's birthmother, Nancy, through a friend. They decided on an independent adoption and got to know one another well during the latter part of Nancy's pregnancy. They did not participate in counseling or work with a professional intermediary. They decided on their own that after the adoption they would keep in touch through letters and pictures, not visitation. However, after placement Nancy decided that she wanted ongoing visitation (it is not unusual for birthparents to decide on increased openness once the baby is born and a reality). Her definition of open adoption was suddenly very different from David and Pam's; both parties had differing expectations for their ongoing relationship. This was very upsetting to David and Pam, and they felt very threatened by visitation, as well as by Nancy herself. A relationship which had been warm and friendly deteriorated into one which was dominated by fear, tension, and misunderstanding.

In looking at this adoption (which is similar to many independent open adoptions that are not facilitated by counseling-based independent adoption programs), it is

obvious that a few key ingredients were missing, which ultimately resulted in some serious problems. There was no adoption intermediary to provide pregnancy counseling and
post-placement grief counseling for Nancy. Nor was there anyone to provide counseling and preparation for both parties
regarding their open adoption relationship. Most adoption
agencies or counseling-based independent, open adoption programs use a written agreement which the participants sign prior
to the adoption and which spells out their ongoing relationship (i.e., the type and frequency of contact over the years).
The intermediary generally also offers mediation counseling
after the adoption if there are any problems or if there need
to be any modifications in this agreement. David, Pam, and
Nancy did not sign an open adoption agreement during Nancy's
pregnancy or afterward.

Pam describes the evolution of the relationship and some
of their feelings and concerns after placement:

> Nancy and her dog Celeste arrived on April 15th, and
> we spent the next 6 weeks getting to know each other
> and preparing for the coming of Kyle. . . . The six weeks
> were spent caring, sharing, and loving each other. On May
> 28 at 8:22 A.M., Kyle was born weighing a healthy 6 lbs.
> 11 oz. We were at the birth and everything went well for
> all. . . .
> Nancy did visit every day after the birth. Originally
> she just wanted to see Kyle once to say goodbye outside
> of hospital surroundings. Six days after the birth Nancy
> returned home. With all the changes in our lives this was
> a joyous, wonderful, and adjusting period for us. . . .
> Nancy had gotten some tickets to a baseball game
> for David's birthday, Aug. 3. Aug. 2 we arrived in the Bay
> Area and stopped by Nancy's house. This was the first time
> we got to see Nancy in her own home. She planned on
> having lunch and having three friends stop by, two of
> whom we already knew. Nancy wanted to talk before they
> arrived, so we sat down and she shared with us that she
> wanted to have ongoing visitation. Well, this not only
> upset me, but she stated she would not sign the adoption

consent papers and would take Kyle from us if we didn't agree to ongoing visitation. Before Kyle's birth, Nancy stated that it would be up to Kyle when he got older if he asked and wanted to see Nancy—would we let him? We said we would. We feel it's Kyle's right to know his birthparents. But I was very upset—almost out of my mind—because she threatened to take Kyle away. . . .

After numerous letters and discussions with Nancy over a period of a few months, as well as one session with a local family counselor, David and Pam decided that they could, in fact, be comfortable with ongoing visitation. But they still felt that their relationship with Nancy was strained as the result of the months of tension and disagreements. At that point, they realized the missing ingredients in their adoption and decided that they all needed professional open adoption counseling in order to work through these problems and develop a more positive relationship. They felt this would be essential for a successful ongoing relationship. So they approached a counseling-based independent adoption program which offers post-adoption counseling. David, Pam, and Nancy participated in two post-adoption counseling sessions which helped them clarify their roles and the realities in open adoption, as well as begin to resolve the problems in their relationship. They decided to participate in additional post-adoption counseling sessions to further cement their relationship.

Nancy expresses her feelings about counseling and the evolution of their relationship:

> . . . In retrospect, we should have had more counseling earlier in our relationship—but we did not and we cannot go backwards. I still feel very good about our relationship, and we have worked through some very difficult times. Over the months since Kyle's birth there have been more good times than bad—although we have had our problems. I'm coming to realize that, as in any long-term relationship between human beings, there are going to be times that we disagree about things, but, if we are

committed to the relationship, then we should be able to work out our differences of opinion. . . .

Pam describes her feelings after counseling:

At the time of this printing, we are still in counseling with Nancy, which has helped reduce the tension for all of us. Adoptive counseling touches places in me which may have otherwise never been exposed—e.g., possession, control, and trust. We are all committed on working on our relationship, which will benefit Kyle in the future.

As we have seen in this chapter, most relationships evolve to positive, loving ones. However, when problems or tensions occur, it is helpful to seek counseling or mediation through a program which specializes in post-adoption services. This is important to the ongoing relationship and to the mental health of the child.

□ 4□

THE PRESCHOOL-AGE CHILD

What is the preschool-age child capable of understanding regarding adoption and specifically open adoption? Alberta Taubert describes three-year-old daughter Jordan's understanding of adoption and birthparents:

> Jordan knows that her birthmother and her family love her. She will tell you that she grew in Christy's tummy and that she gets her curly hair from Christy. I believe that while she, of course, doesn't fully understand adoption that she does have a positive feeling about it. We videotaped the placement, and Jordan will watch it saying "that's my birthmother." As she grows I think it will become very special to her. She will see Christy crying and know how difficult it was for her; she will also *see* our empathy for Christy and our joy at finally becoming a family. . . .

Discussing Adoption with the Child

Frequently, adoptive parents think a preschool-age child cannot "understand" adoption. Some parents wait until the child is preadolescent, adolescent, or even adult to "tell him he was adopted," with tragic results (the child or adult feels he has lived a lie and this causes serious damage to his sense of trust in his parents). Of course, the preschool child does not have an adult understanding of adoption, but he can *begin* to absorb that which is shared with him.

Dear Birthmother refers to a "building block" process in which parents begin discussing adoption from infancy—a "gradual and natural approach." When an infant hears "I love you," he has no concept of what the word "love" means. However, he gradually internalizes it as a positive word associated with tender holding and loving facial expressions. In like fashion, adoption vocabulary becomes internalized in a positive manner.

With the young child, adoption should be a household word—a natural subject in the home. The parents should openly discuss adoption with the child, rather than waiting for the child to ask questions. *The responsibility for bringing up the subject of adoption rests with the parents, not the child.* As noted in *Dear Birthmother,* "Many of our two-year-olds tell people, 'I 'dopted' with the same understanding as when they hold up two fingers in response to questions of age." The child may not grasp what it means, but he knows that it is about him and that it is something positive (from the positive, happy way in which his parents use the word). This is an important first building block to increased understanding later.

From the start, children should be told about growing in someone else's womb. This is particularly significant to children 3-5 years old, an age when children normally want to know where babies come from. It is both important and necessary to discuss this and incorporate it into the adoption story. In fact, it is an integral part of the adoption story; one cannot discuss adoption without explaining that the child grew in someone else's womb. Some adoptive parents (assuming that their child is too young to understand) have left out this part of the story in explaining adoption by simply stating that the child "came from the agency." This has been even more confusing to the child, resulting in anxieties and nightmares, because everyone else grew in their mommy's womb but he came from "the agency" (which to a young child must seem as bizarre as coming from outer space). In this stage of "magical thinking," these young children internalize information, truly believing they magically sprouted from the agency, like a Cabbage Patch doll.

Becca Marsh relates that she discussed adoption from infancy with her son, and she recalls his understanding at age four-and-a-half:

> I wanted him to be very familiar and comfortable with the word so that his realization of its meaning would be gradual and not traumatic. I think we have been successful. We have had several talks on the subject. When we were waiting to get our second baby, one of my good friends was expecting a baby. J.D., of course, was full of questions about why I was not getting big and fat like my friend, if we were getting a baby, too. I explained to him about birthmothers giving birth and then the Mama raises the baby. I told him that for some babies the birthmother and Mama were the same person, but adopted babies had a separate birthmother and Mama. He was 4½ at the time, and he seemed to understand and accept this.

Actually, in our combined experience, we have found that the preschool child understands *more* than most adoption experts believe. This is because these experts/therapists are primarily working with children adopted through traditional adoption, where the unknowns and abstract concepts are truly difficult to comprehend. We recall one 2½-year-old child who verbalized "My birthmother—she not know me?" Even at the early age of 2½ this child could grasp the concept of birthmother, as well as the fact that her birthmother was no longer part of her life. We strongly believe that children are capable of understanding much more than we have given them credit for in the past.

Open Adoption Facilitates Understanding

As Alberta Taubert indicates, her three-year-old daughter, Jordan, is able to appropriately use the term birthmother and to realize that she grew in Christy's womb and, in fact, got her curly hair from Christy. Of course, Jordan only has an elementary understanding of adoption, and her knowledge will grow during the school-age years. But she has an appropriate level of understanding for her age and comfortably uses adoption terminology. This is largely because Jordan has an open adoption. Christy is real to Jordan (rather than an abstract concept); Christy is someone who is part of her life and who Jordan sees on a regular basis. That makes adoption easier to comprehend.

Openness facilitates the rate at which adoption information is absorbed by the preschool-age child. Jordan is not confused—quite the opposite. She knows who her mommy is (Alberta), but she also knows who her birthmother is. Because she personally knows Christy and sees her periodically, this is not confusing; rather, it is *real*. Rather than dealing with the abstract, she is receiving concrete information to process. As Yvonne, mother of a four-year-old and a six-year-old, states, "I think the openness is helping them understand the concept of adoption." In addition, this age child needs *concrete* evidence of the birthparents caring; physical contact and gifts provide that assurance.

Jeryl Simms, the adoptive mother of two girls, ages 3 and 5, comments that open adoption means "Being able to talk more openly to the girls and being more knowledgeable about their birthmothers and about adoption itself. We can answer more of their questions, and it makes things so much more personal." She notes that she frequently talks to her daughters about growing in their birthmothers' wombs. In these discussions with Ashley, age 5, "We can talk about Karin (her birthmother) as a person she knows and cares about—not some imagined person—and it makes her feel better."

Another adoptive mother, Laurie Morkert, recalls that when she was discussing where babies come from with her 3½-year-old daughter, Cara responded immediately, "But I didn't come from your tummy, I came from Ann's." Laurie notes, "Needless to say, I was amazed at the depth of her understanding." When Cara was five years old and in kindergarten, the children were asked to draw a family picture. "Cara wanted to draw herself as a baby in Ann's arms, and Ann and Greg (her birthparents) were holding hands. I was on Ann's left and my husband was on Greg's right." To Cara her family picture included both sets of parents and demonstrated her grasp of their reality in her life.

In contrast, in traditional adoption the child hears the term adoption and may know he grew in someone else's womb, but since everything is unknown it is "unreal," harder to comprehend, and confusing (frequently resulting in anxieties, as well as fantasies about the unknown and mysterious birthmother). Critics of open adoption have hypothesized that open adoption would be confusing to the young child. But in our experience in observing families with open adoption, we have found quite the opposite to be true. The children of open adoption are, in fact, faring better than those with traditional adoption because open adoption makes adoption *real* and, therefore, understandable.

Sensitivity on the part of adoptive parents is certainly crucial as sharing of information occurs. Messages that are simple in nature are most appropriate for this age group. Too many details may confuse a young child. We encourage parents to provide honest and open communication, while adding details as they deem appropriate for their child. For example, in discussing the birthmother with whom contact is maintained, the parents must clearly explain to the child that the birthmother is *his birthmother* and that he grew in her womb. It is inappropriate (and will cause serious problems later) if the birthmother is introduced to the child as an "aunt" or special friend. In these situations, when the child later learns that who he thought was "Aunt Susie" is now his birthmother, he can become very angry, as well as confused about adoption.

As open communication takes place within the family, parents discover that their young children convey a rather complex level of understanding. When Katherine was 3½, she asked what her birthfather's name was. Her mother was stunned about the question as she had not explicitly introduced the father concept yet, nor had she used that vocabulary with her youngster. Their focus had been on the birthmother. She was most impressed with her child's reasoning. A few months later, Katherine again asked to know his name, and her mom realized that an unnecessary fixation was taking place. She obtained the birthfather's name. Katherine

Jennifer, age 3, writes her birthmother.

Tyler, age 3½, thanks Dierdre,
her birthmother, for her Christmas gifts.

used it matter of factly when it suited her. The fixation had dissolved with the knowledge.

Where there is ongoing correspondence, the preschool child is quite capable of understanding who his parents are writing to and participating in the correspondence himself (remember, the birthmother is a *real* person to him). The child usually communicates with a drawing or else dictates a letter, which mom or dad writes for him. The two drawings on the previous page are examples of how preschoolers participate in communication.

When Helen was 4¼ she dictated a letter she wanted to write. Her message was as follows:

> Elaine, I really, really miss you. Someday you can invite us to visit you.
>
> *Love, Helen.*

She then drew the picture below to reflect that imagined visit. She explained to her mother that "Elaine's apartment in New York is #1. When I see Elaine, I will give her a big hug. Elaine will say 'Hi, Helen.' Elaine will feel happy. Helen will feel happy. Mommy will feel happy." Helen's mother asked, "What will make us happy?" Helen responded, "Elaine."

Grief in Preschoolers

The realization and experience of loss is demonstrated by adopted children at earlier ages than previously believed. The different manifestations of grief are evidenced by the children—we see denial, sadness, and anger. Jennifer's story reflects how denial came into play for this child:

At age 4½ Jennifer began to emphatically say that she had not grown in Gloria's (birthmother) womb. Over time, Jennifer's mom had explained her adoption story in simple terms, including that Jennifer had grown in Gloria's womb. Jennifer's denial of this reality puzzled her mom for awhile. Suddenly a flash of memory reminded her of a similar incident shared by another adoptive parent many years before. Adopted children sometimes deny their adopted status because they love their parents and wish they had been born to them. They also grieve the loss of the mother in whose womb they grew.

Jennifer's mom relates:

> Once I suspected the connection between her words and her feelings, I spoke with Jennifer. I kneeled down so she and I could have eye contact and physical contact. I anticipated an emotional exchange. I reflected to her that lately she had been saying she had not grown in Gloria's womb. I asked her if what she was saying was that she wished she had grown in my womb. With great emotion and tenderness, she nodded and hugged me. I told her that I also wished she had grown in my womb, but that she had, in fact, grown in Gloria's womb, and that I was okay with that. A few days later she was back to having grown in Gloria's womb and saying that Gloria had given birth to her. She had been validated, and she was assisted in processing her feelings. Another intimate bridging occurred, further cementing our relationship and our reality.

It is important for parents to recognize behavior related to the grief experience—a grief experience that intertwines the two mother's in the child's life. Gaining a sense of well being about one's reality becomes vital for the child. Using messages of love, such as letters, from the birthmother helps pave the way for acceptance to occur. We will further discuss grief in children in the next chapter.

Expressions of Love

As we have seen, preschool children will naturally accept and feel comfortable with open adoption if it is handled in an open and honest manner, incorporating the birthmother into his life as a real person. When this happens the child will express love and affection for the birthmother, just as he expresses affection to other people who are close to him (e.g., grandparents). It is typical for the child to hug the birthmother when she arrives, to sit in her lap, to say "I love you," etc. This can be somewhat threatening to adoptive parents if they have not fully accepted the adoption realities which we have previously discussed (e.g., the reality of two sets of parents).

Adoptive parents should not feel they have to compete with the birthparents or to automatically assume that the child loves the birthmother *more* because she is his birthmother. The child's adoptive parents are his *parents*, but he can also love and care for his birthparents. The adoptive parents must be able to understand and accept this in order to not feel threatened by demonstrations of affection toward the birthparents. They should not get into some sort of competition with the birthparents, but, rather, feel comfortable with and accept each other's roles in the child's life. Insight and understanding helps, as well as making conscious efforts to overcome any feelings of threat.

Barbara Alleruzzo shares her feelings regarding this issue:

> At times Marion (birthmother) will refer to Luciano as "our son" or his birthgrandparents will sign letters "Grandma & Grandpa." I am sensitive to hear these things and know that the older my son gets the more possessive I am. I think it would be easier emotionally to pretend the birthparents don't exist. But, realistically, I feel blessed my son has such a loving birthfamily. I just have to remind myself not to let my possessiveness get in the way.

Betty Wunsche shares her feelings regarding her daughter's affection toward her birthmother, acknowledging that jealousy can occur towards other people beside the birthmother:

> I know when we meet and Kirsten is affectionate with Tina (her birthmother), I feel a tiny bit of jealousy. But sometimes I feel the same with Gaby, a particularly loving friend of ours.

Jeanne Etter describes her feelings of jealousy (and eventually acceptance of the birthmother's role) when her daughter's birthmother, Mary, came to visit when Angela was 16 months old:

> I came into the family room to hear Mary saying to Angela, "That pin could hurt you. Give it to Mama." I walked out, hurt and resentful. I later talked to a close friend, saying I felt like Mary was trying to be the mother when she had said she wouldn't. My friend told me bluntly, "She *is* a mother. She is Angela's birthmother and you can never undo that." I realized that I had a choice of feeling defensive or of changing my thinking. It didn't make me any less Angela's mother because Mary was one too. Much as we would like sometimes to make it possible, you can't divorce a child or divorce someone's child from them the way you can divorce your spouse.

Jeryl Simms and her daughters, Ashley, age 5, and Heather, age 3, engage in ongoing visitation with both birthmothers. They see Ashley's birthmother and birthgrandmother several times a year, and they visit with Heather's birthmother a few times a year. They also speak on the phone periodically, and Heather's birthmother sends Heather postcards every few weeks (she began doing this after Jeryl mentioned once on the phone that Heather enjoys getting mail). Jeryl comments on her feelings about the birthmothers and her daughters' affection towards them:

> I do not feel threatened by the birthmothers. I know they feel good about us raising their children, and I know

they love the girls. I'm glad they do, and I'm glad the girls will always know their birthmothers love them. When Ashley was 4, she once told me right before she went to sleep that she wished she was a baby again so she could go live in Karin's (her birthmother) house. It sent a pain through my heart, but I knew she didn't mean she didn't want to live with us—but, rather, she looked at it as a fun and new experience for her (she had just spent a weekend at her cousin's house for the first time and thoroughly enjoyed it).

I really am thankful that the girls care about their birthmothers. There are so many adoptive children growing up with bad feelings about their birthmothers because of feelings of rejection. I feel with the relationships we have already established my children will not go through that.

It is also important to point out that the birthparents are *prime* people in the child's life. The child knows that he grew in the birthmother's womb, and he feels a *very* strong bond with her, even if he only sees her every year or two. There is an intensity to their relationship, even in the case of the preschool-age child. So it is normal for the child to demonstrate love and affection for the birthmother.

Visitation

We are familiar with some situations in which the adoptive parents agree to visitation for the first one to two years, when they feel the child won't understand who the birthparents are. They then want to cut it off because they fear that it will be confusing to the child. We certainly acknowledge that these parents have good intentions, not wanting their children to be damaged by contact. But they must be able to recognize that, in fact, the children fare okay, even when there are frequent visits. Furthermore, if the birthparent is phased out, issues of abandonment can surface for the child (at that time and in later years).

It is important to underscore that ongoing contact will not be confusing to the child, unless the parents themselves are uncomfortable with visits and, as a result, the child senses this. If the parents feel threatened by the concept of two sets of parents, ongoing physical contact will produce anxiety. The child will sense these feelings, even if the parents do not verbalize their fears. In addition, children receive other cues from their parents. When these are positive, the nature of the contact consistently is taken in stride as natural, rather than as an unusual phenomenon.

Where families decide to terminate visits, it seems to be the *adoptive parents'* "issues" and insecurities (regarding two sets of parents) which lead to this decision, not the child's. In fact, they may be unable to see beyond their own insecurities to be able to recognize what is in the child's best interest. We have consistently witnessed this with families who have chosen to cease physical contact.

With continued visits, the question quickly arises of what to call the birthparents. In our experience, it is preferable for the child and parents to call the birthparents by their first names. However, the child should be clearly told that this person is his birthmother, that he grew in her womb, etc. Preschool-age children (including pre-verbal children) should be prepared for each visit, with a simple explanation of adoption and birthparents. Too often, children are handled casually, because of their age and parents' assumptions regarding their limited comprehension of adoption; instead, children need special assistance in order to facilitate understanding. In terms of the actual visit itself, there should not be a lot of physical contact with the birthparents (hugging, kissing, etc.) unless the child himself seems to invite this. The adults should take their cues from the child, rather than pushing the child into intimacy which may seem frightening or uncomfortable to him. Preschool children also demonstrate varied responses to visits. Some children seem happy and casual regarding visits and others may show some anxiety or stress (e.g., nightmares). Whatever the reaction, it is important for parents to continue to explain to the child his relationship to the birthparents and his permanence in his adoptive family. Frequent contact, trust, familiarity, and permanence go hand in hand with the child's developing understanding of adoption. The message of love and caring will be internalized, even at the preverbal stage.

Judy Albrecht shares her experiences with ongoing visitation and a preschooler's understanding of open adoption:

> Around Emily's fourth birthday, we made our yearly trip to see Katherine (Emily's birthmother). During the visit Emily was looking at pictures of her and Katherine right after her birth—one was of her when she had just emerged from Katherine's womb. Emily said, "You are my birthmom. You gave me my Birthday, but this is my Mom (me). For an instant I perceived anguish on Katherine's face and then comfort. It was an intense moment of redefinition. I simultaneously felt empathy for Katherine and an affirmation of my parenting role. I think we all bonded more that day as we moved along the continuum of grief, peace, and connectedness.

Infertility Revisited

In the preschool years, particularly when parents first discuss with the child that he grew in someone else's womb, they confront their infertility once more. In discussing pregnancy and birth, old feelings regarding their infertility (which they may have assumed were long forgotten) can resurface. As we have discussed previously, grief is not a one-time event but reappears at various intervals. It is essential for adoptive parents to be prepared for these feelings and to understand that they are normal.

In addition, open adoption, in particular, involves confrontation with infertility on an ongoing basis. If parents are engaged in visitation with the birthmother, there is a constant reminder of their infertility and her biological relationship with the child. In order to feel comfortable with visitation, adoptive parents must have come to terms with their infertility. Otherwise, the visits can be too painful and reopen old wounds.

Two adoptive mothers who engage in ongoing contact and who also have resolved their feelings about their infertility comment on the impact of visitation on infertility. Laurie

Morkert notes, "It closes the wounds and allows you to go on with your life. Openness never permits you to develop some fantasy that this child is 'only mine' [as in a birth experience]." Betty Wunsche no longer experiences the pain of infertility, but she can identify with the pain and loss of the birthparent experience. Betty, who visits with her daughter's birthmother, Tina, every year or two, notes, "Tina experienced the 'giving life' or birth, but I experience mothering, which she does not. I don't think I open my wounds of 'loss' [the loss of a biological child] when I see Tina, but I experience them empathically for her because I take Kirsten home with me [after visits]."

We have found that adoptive parents who have contact with birthparents better process their infertility experience and reach a point of acceptance. Through confrontation with reality, these parents emotionally progress along the grief continuum to a more peaceful resolution. The competition between the fertile and infertile seems to diminish and finally evaporate. Each becomes affirmed for his/her role in the child's life. Fertility no longer plays the role of self-esteem-giver or -robber.

Deanna shares her perspective. "Being allowed to grieve the loss through infertility allows me to grow beyond it, to accept it, and to know it's OK. I'm OK. Meeting Brooke's birthmother, in fact, made me feel whole; she filled the part of me that was void by choosing life for Brooke and by choosing us to be her parents." The Mials adopted two brothers and have maintained contact with their birthmother over the years. Missy Mial expresses her feelings, "Contrary to what I used to think possible, my infertility 'wounds' have healed. A major contributing factor in this is that I am so content as a parent . . . the openness has given me that."

Discipline

In most cases there are differences in how the two sets of parents view discipline. These differences become more obvious in situations where there is ongoing visitation. It is not uncommon for the birthmother to think "I wouldn't discipline him that way," or even to interfere in how the adoptive parents are disciplining the child. However, in placing a child for adoption, the birthparents must understand and accept that they are "giving up" the parenting role to the adoptive parents. They must allow the adoptive parents to parent the child—and, yes, even to make mistakes, as all parents do. The birthparents must not interfere, just as they probably would not interfere in the way other close friends or relatives raise their children. They must be able to trust the parents enough to let them parent.

Jacklyn Schofield, a birthmother who has been engaging in ongoing visitation for four years, discusses her feelings about visitation, expressions of love, and discipline:

> Open adoption . . . how could it be anything but wonderful? I just came from my son's fourth birthday party. Is it painful for me to see him? He is adorable, charming, self-confident, happy . . . all the traits I wanted him to have. No, seeing him isn't painful or awkward. On the contrary, it confirms that he is indeed becoming everything I dreamed he could become because I had the courage to choose adoption. Gavin's family has become my family and in turn my family has become part of their family. Visiting is always a happy occasion that leaves each of us with fond memories.
>
> At first I worried that somehow they would interpret my interest in visiting to mean I wanted to raise Gavin myself. That's why open adoption is so important. We have grown to trust one another because we know one another. They know that I love Gavin and that I love them too. They have learned that I would never jeopardize that trust. Robert and Karen have been able to share their dreams for Gavin with me, along with the life they are creating, so that I can share in their joy.
>
> A second milestone in my adoption probably came as Gavin grew to recognize me as an important person in his life. Robert and Karen have talked about me to Gavin and included pictures of me in his everyday life from day one. So it's not surprising that he recognized me from

an early age. Naturally it thrills me when I come to visit and he greets me with a hug and kiss. Recently he climbed on my lap, put his arms around me, and said "I love you— I love your being my birthmother." Early on he was very shy when I would arrive and then warm up as the visit wore on. When he first began to acknowledge me right away it was great for me but a little difficult for Karen. In her heart she knew Gavin was clear that she was his mother but there was still that fear deep down that somehow he would know I was his "real" mother. Together we talked about it so that I could understand her fears and not take offense at them. Through our friendship she could be assured that I recognized her position as Gavin's mother.

Today Karen is able to encourage Gavin's affection toward me without any fears. Gavin can tell me he loves me and she knows that doesn't mean that he prefers me to her. I believe the time we have shared together has enlightened all of us about children's understanding of adoption. Gavin understands who I am and clearly feels close to me, but whenever he needs "mothering," like when he's not feeling well, or feeling insecure, or falls down, he goes directly to Karen. Sure, sometimes I'm envious when that happens, but that was a reality I faced when I made my adoption decision. It's not harder to see Gavin rely on Karen than it is to think about it at home. It's just part of adoption.

Today open adoption is not a hospital event alone, it is a lifelong process for everyone involved. Consequently, I believe it is important to choose parents that share the same parenting ideals that you have. I admire Robert and Karen's parenting. Even so, there are occasions during visits when I think to myself, "Why do they let him get away with that? I would handle that situation differently." Do I feel I should say something? Thanks to good counseling, I had addressed that issue in my mind before it actually occurred. My role in Gavin's life is as his birthmother, not his parent. I chose the best parents

I could find to fill that role, now it was up to me to let them do that. Sure it's hard from time to time, but it's not any harder than watching my good friends discipline their children in a way that I don't approve of. I wouldn't dream of criticizing my friends' parenting, so why should that be any different from the friendship I have established with Robert and Karen? It's not, and therefore I don't criticize their parenting.

Our experience has consistently demonstrated that birth-parents are respectful of the adoptive parents' parenting role. Discipline is one major ingredient within this.

□ 5 □

THE SCHOOL-AGE CHILD
PART I

Today, even the children of traditional adoption usually grow up with the knowledge of being adopted. Typically, however, questions which arise about their adoption have no answers. The closed adoption system results in parents being given scarce or no information about their children's origins. The belief, of course, has traditionally been that none of this would be necessary, especially if the family is a well-functioning one. Furthermore, it has been believed that adoption is basically a time limited event—that once the adoption takes place, there is no difference between an adoptive family and a "mainstream" family.

Kirk expounded on the hazards of such a position in his book *Adoptive Kinship*. He called this process "denial of difference" and remarked on how detrimental this was to the family. Adoptive families indeed do deal with special issues related to adoption which are not typically found in mainstream families. As Wishard and Wishard so aptly stated in their book *The Grafted Tree*, adoptive parents have all the joys and responsibilities of parenthood in addition to the special issues of adoption.

How then can one find a positive balance for not over-focusing on adoption while acknowledging its role in the lives of those involved? We have found that clear and honest communication becomes a vital ingredient for negotiating this very complex experience. Throughout the school-age years, children continue to develop their understanding of adoption. This is especially true when building blocks are used whereby information is shared in gradual dosages. As parents develop the skills of communication and their comfort level increases, children feel free to comment on and ask questions about adoption matters.

The practice of open adoption embodies the gathering and sharing of information. Parents are better equipped to respond to their children so energy doesn't have to be expended in wondering. As children receive answers, they demonstrate the capacity to integrate the information and move on. As we discussed with preschool-age children, concrete information facilitates understanding during the school-age years as well. A simple question like "what was my birth-mother's name" can be a powerful emotional bonding opportunity between adoptive parent and child when an answer is provided comfortably and truthfully. The comfort level reflected from parent to child contributes to the trust and love bonds between them. As Amber, age 8, once said to her Mom, "I really am glad you are my mother because you understand about adoption." What a confirmation for the process of open communications and sharing of available information.

In observing the children of open adoption compared to the children of closed adoption, we clearly see that they are faring better from a mental health point of view. They have concrete information about themselves, as well as access to ongoing information over the years. They do not have to be confused by, or obsessed with, unanswered questions or fantasies. They accept the relationship with their birthparents as extended family members as natural and normal. In addition, as we will discuss later in this chapter, children with closed adoptions also benefit from opening up their adoptions during the school-age years.

Communication: Questions or Lack Thereof

It is interesting to note that many adoptive parents report that their children ask no adoption-related questions. In some cases it may be true that the child really has a low level of curiosity. In these situations, it becomes the parents' responsibility to pave the way for future questions. This can be done by making statements or posing questions regarding adoption.

Some examples would be:

"Before we adopted you, we lived in Washington."

"I bet your birthmother is thinking about you today" (on the child's birthday).

"Do you want to know what your birthmother looked like?"

Speaking naturally about adoption gives the child the message that when he wishes to talk about adoption it is OK. Today there are excellent books designed for children, such as *Why Was I Adopted?*, *How It Feels To Be Adopted*, *I'm Still Me*, *Adoption is for Always*, and *Becky's Special Family*. Having these as part of one's library is another way to convey this message. The open adoption experience (combined with tuned-in adoptive parents) has demonstrated that children ask many questions. When Kirsten was seven years old she asked her mother, "Why did Tina get pregnant with me when she wasn't going to keep me?" This is a fairly complex question. Questions regarding core adoption issues begin early. It doesn't matter how many questions are expressed or when these occur. The vital ingredient is that children learn early that it is perfectly acceptable to communicate about adoption.

This is still the case even when parents don't have answers to the questions or don't even have access to these. When Bree Clark was six years old, his mother, Barbara, asked him what he would say if he were able to meet his birthmother. He immediately responded, "Hi! I don't remember the first time I met you, but I understand why you did what you did and I'm happy." The immediacy of his response demonstrated to Barbara how much processing Bree was doing in an ongoing fashion regarding his adoption. When permission is given to verbalize, children express complex thoughts and emotions.

It is important to learn from adult adoptees who share that it was often difficult to ask the millions of questions they had, both for fear of hurting their parents and because they felt it was disloyal to their parents. The self-denial of these adoptees still exists in huge proportions. A frequently represented element is fixation because of a lack of answers.

Children of open adoption are spared this burden. Answers are readily available or easily obtained as the need arises. Sometimes the answer is not as critical as the validation for asking in the first place—the message being that having curiosity is normal and acceptable, and, furthermore, that efforts will be made to obtain answers.

The more the adoptive parents acknowledge that the child has a history that occurred preadoption, the more they are able to integrate that reality into their family system. They then find it easier to convey the adoption comfort which leads invariably to adoption communication. One adoptive mother notes, "Since our children have had contact with their birthmothers, we have sat down several times to go through all of our 'vital stats' about their birthfamilies that the agency gave us." She feels this has had a positive impact on her children and the family as a whole. The children know they can ask questions openly.

School-Age Children's Understanding of Adoption and Loss

Open adoption affords the child the opportunity of turning his adoption experience into one of *concrete* elements. During the preschool years he has demonstrated some fairly sophisticated levels of understanding, as previously stated. During the early school-age years he is broadening and refining this understanding. He still does not comprehend the moral issues associated with adoption, such as the judgmental stance of society regarding both unmarried parenthood and birthparenthood. What he does understand is that he did not grow in his adoptive mother's womb and that he did grow in his birthmother's womb. He is *struggling* to understand cognitively the words conveying that his birthmother's decision was made with his welfare in mind.

What is surfacing with greater intensity at this age is the conflict embodying the theme of love vs. rejection—"If she loved me so much, why did she give me away?" This is an ongoing struggle for adopted children, whether they verbalize it or not. This is also the ongoing struggle of adopted adults

as they express one of the central questions in adoption—
"Why was I adopted?" The underlying theme behind this question is, "Was the adoption decision based on love or rejection?" The closed adoption system provides no avenue for confirmation, and the struggle continues until a search is completed. Through contact, resolution becomes possible.

With open adoption, these issues can be processed over time with evidence of love and clarification. As Kirsten, age 8, stated, "Brent (birthfather) sent me a picture he made himself. I know he loves me from this." Stacy, age 12, recounts that when she met her birthmother, she asked her if she *still* loved her. When her birthmother said she did, Stacy "felt real good." She does not have the need to ask her this question each time she sees her. If the need arises again, she knows she will feel comfortable asking again.

During the school-age years, children begin to understand that their communities often do not perceive adoption as a positive quality. Other children ask them if they lived in orphanages—symbols of abandoned children. Statements like "I'm sorry" when adoptive status is mentioned reinforces the negative. Young school-age children cannot quite make sense of these comments but quickly pick up their negative nuances. Thus, they often begin to protect the revelation of being adopted, without fully understanding why.

Children of open adoption become more empowered to deal with these situations, as they have information available that refutes the negatives. It still is a burden but often a better managed one. They have a greater sense of well-being knowing they are actively loved and remembered. Bree, age 10, shares that the children at school think being adopted is akin to Orphan Annie's experience. They ask him if he was in an orphanage. When asked where his "real" parents are, he says, "They're living at my home." Jill, an adoptive mom, conveys how early negative attitudes are developed:

> My neighbor, Lea, has a daughter, Carlie, who is 8 years old. Carlie told my adopted daughter, Jenna (age 7) how "lucky" she (Jenna) was to have a mother! Lea thought her daughter had said something wonderful—

I was appalled! My child has two mothers who love her and we are the lucky ones to have her in our lives! I am sure my daughter spent some time trying to make sense out of why she should be lucky to have a mother. For children, this is a given. The underlying message, of course, was that she had been rejected the first time around! Since we are involved with open adoption, we are able to keep reinforcing how loved she is by all of us. We continue to show her evidence through many forms of contact. Still, outsiders' attitudes do affect her willingness to be "public" about adoption on a regular basis. She learned early that while we feel adoption is a positive experience, society doesn't always support that position.

Something we have done is use the technique David Kirk mentions in his book, *Adoptive Kinship*. He talks about how outsiders just don't understand. This is the message we help our daughter absorb—there are a lot of people who just don't understand adoption. Very often Jenna will say that phrase herself when she has to deal with individuals who "don't get it." This seems to be comforting in that she knows something others don't!

Grief Issues for School-Age Children

Emotionally and cognitively, school-age children demonstrate a heightened awareness of the fact that they have experienced a major loss through adoption. In the 1970's, the field of adoption began to recognize the loss pertaining to adopted persons. However, usually this was alluded to only in relation to the adult experience. During the early 80's, adoption professionals began to recognize that feelings of loss started in early childhood. As a matter of fact, we see evidence that grief is experienced by children at a preverbal level. Some professionals believe that even *in utero* the child senses the impending separation. Thomas Verny, author of *The Secret Life of the Unborn Child* examines at length the *in utero* experience and its impact over one's lifetime. Some professionals subscribe to the philosophy that the loss experience begins upon separation in infancy. Whatever one's philosophical and experiential position, it is generally accepted that loss is an integral part of being adopted.

Manifestations of the grief reactions that result include all the typical stages of grieving, among them—denial, anger, sadness, and self-blame. One of the most frequently identified grief-related behaviors is displaced anger. It is evidenced (but not limited to) during the preschool- and school-age years. The child dumps his anger, often at the rage level, typically on the adoptive mother (after all, she is the mother figure). She becomes the object of his wrath. Adoptive mothers often report relief at being able to identify this pattern, as they can better address it and help the child process his feelings.

Lori, age 6, said, "When I get mad at you, I am mad at her. She gave me away." This is often a circular pathway that revolves around the mother issue. Through openness the child can better be assisted in the verification of the continued love and caring of his birthmother. When doubt strikes, outreach can be made to help the child through each developmental stage, involving the birthparents to whatever degree helps the child.

Jane, an adoptive mother, had recently become aware of grief issues in children. She reflected that Elizabeth, her 8-year-old, sometimes cried for unexplained reasons. Wanting to explore this with Elizabeth, she said, "Sometimes adopted kids feel sad because they have lost something." Elizabeth flashed back with intensity, "I've lost *someone!*" Jane was stunned by the immediacy of the response and the emotion that accompanied it. It confirmed for her that her daughter, indeed, was dealing with adoption-related grief. This exchange allowed them to communicate further.

In our work with adopted adults who experienced closed adoption we have often witnessed how this displaced anger has interfered with bonding with the adoptive parents. Barriers to intimacy were created, as a result—not just with the adoptive parents, but in other relationships as well. We have come to realize that this issue is multifaceted. Anger makes for distance, and distance makes for reduced risk of future losses. Adoptees frequently are fearful of losing another meaningful relationship. Rather than risk this loss, they don't allow it to occur in the first place. Time after time, we have seen adopted adults redefine their relationships with their adoptive parents after a search for birthparents is completed. As the healing process occurs between them and their birthparents, they become freed up to finally establish intimate bonds with others—especially significant others. In adoption circles it is typical to hear comments regarding how much closer adoptive parents and their children become after a search is completed. This strengthened intimacy has to do with the elimination of walls often psychologically and emotionally built by the adoptee himself.

Through open adoption, the children do not have to create the barriers to intimacy. Their grief and loss issues are dealt with better. Displaced anger can be rerouted into a more productive use of energy. We are not saying that these elements disappear completely, but we see a much diminished incidence and intensity. Children who experience loss have a hard time trusting. When the loss is directly confronted and allowed to be processed, the trust level is enhanced. Only through trust can intimacy be established.

Another manifestation of grief in children is self-blame. They believe that they were too ugly, too noisy, unlovable, and so on. It is important to redirect the children so they do not expend a lot of energy tearing down their self-esteem. Through contact with birthparents, both sets of parents are able to provide the "why" data and avoid self-blame. Emily Albrecht, age 6½, was recently discussing adoption with Judy, her mother. She suddenly began to cry and said, "After all, it wasn't my fault." Judy responded, "That's right."

Parents who help their children through these episodes with an understanding of the grief process dramatically contribute to the positive processing of emotions. It must be acknowledged that witnessing these emotions in our children is painful. However, parental empathy paves the way for healing and further bonding. The child is allowed to feel his pain and be validated. He can then move on emotionally.

Birthparents involved with open adoption are able to let the child know directly that the adoption decision had nothing to do with his personal attributes—that no matter what child would have been born, the outcome would have been the same, given the birthparents' circumstances at that time. This opportunity for direct reality basing is tremendously helpful to children. This impacts both in the development of understanding and the emotional processing of loss. Again, the availability of the concrete message, vs. abstract suppositions, enhances the child's ability to move on in a more positive direction.

Grief and loss are part of any adoption experience. What we have seen in open adoption is a greater degree of comfort and peace with one's reality when contact is part of the adoption experience. Incremental resolution and acceptance become the outcome. Katherine often lamented that she did not live with her birthmother. When she was 9, she expressed explicitly that she was at greater peace about this. It no longer appeared to eat at her. Her acting out behavior (loaded with anger) had diminished. This does not mean her fantasy has totally disappeared, but, through discussion and emotional processing, she grows towards a healthier integration of her reality.

The goal is to acknowledge the loss and to work towards an experience that brings about healing through connectedness. This leads to healthier acceptance.

The grief work for adopted children is an ongoing process. As we have discussed, through open adoption, children are able to work through their grief more effectively. Judy Albrecht shares her observations of Emily:

> I have always looked at our connections with Emily's birthfamily as incremental grief work. Up until last year we probably witnessed pre-language grief, and we just had faith that Emily would work it out. Last year when she turned 6 and we visited Katherine (birthmother), we saw for the first time a lack of stressors for Emily.
>
> When she was a baby, after the visits she often had a temperature. At ages 3 and 4 she demonstrated approach/avoidance behaviors. Before the visits, she would spend a lot of time selecting which dress she would wear and make statements that showed excitement and

anticipation. She would alternately say, "This is not my idea, it's your idea."

Last year she showed peaceful calm before and during the visit. She interacted more physically with Katherine than ever before. Her comfort level was obviously high. At each step of the way, we have seen Emily grow in her processing of adoption. Up until that point, I feel that Emily was looking for a relation—how she fit, whom she looked like, and what her birthmother was all about. We now reached a turning point where Emily was ready for a relationship.

When asked how she felt to witness this change, Judy quickly responded, "Relieved! As she bonds with Katherine, she bonds with us."

When is the Right Time to Share a Picture, Gift, Letter?

Adoptive parents have reported personal comfort with letters and pictures exchanged with birthparents. They sometimes worry about what the appropriate schedule is for sharing these with a child. Often expressed concerns are that the child may be confused or negatively impacted. It has been our experience that children are pleased to hear a letter read to them even in the preschool years and that pictures are admired and then dealt with casually. These vehicles of communication have facilitated further communication within the family over time.

Once children know there are pictures, they tend to ask to see them whenever they feel the need. The typical behavior is very relaxed and matter-of-fact. Some children display the picture of their birthparent(s) and/or siblings in their bedroom. Amy, age 12, recently told her mother that she took a picture of her sibling (being raised by her birthmother) to show at school. She was very matter-of-fact and just wanted to share this information with her classmates.

We have found that some parents, unsure about appropriate timing, have withheld information of pictures and letters from their children. When they are finally ready to share these with their children they encounter surprise on the children's part that these were not shared before. The message seems to be "What is the big deal?"

As parents become more knowledgeable about all that adoption entails, it is important for them to explore their feelings about these links to the birthparent. Often, it is one more dimension of open acknowledgement of their reality—this reality being that their child has another set of parents. This also forces them to confront the areas of infertility, entitlement, and so on. Once parents have an opportunity to explore their feelings, needs, and perceptions, they can then be guided regarding the use of these forms of communication.

Children learn about adoption and its meaning from their parents' words, nonverbal messages, and emotional signals. Much of adoption communication tends to be too abstract for a small child who has no concept of what it takes to be a parent. Furthermore, he has no notion of the stresses and pressures associated with an unplanned pregnancy and how that relates to his present situation. So, much of early parental communication conveys how loved the child is by birthparents— these often elusive beings, hard to visualize without concrete cues.

As teaching about adoption takes place, it is very natural to couch it with visual aids appropriate for children's developmental stages. Thus, a picture is a level of reality that allows a preschool and school-age child to visualize birthparents. A letter gives a concrete message from a real person—words from that person him- or herself. A gift also presents the concrete for a child dealing with so many abstract concepts.

Again, as in so many adoption-related matters, the key seems to relate to parental comfort. In addition to this key ingredient, we have found that parents' knowledge and understanding about adoption also are important elements. June adopted her child, Diane, as an infant. Their adoption was closed. When Diane was nine her birthmother, Maria, approached the agency seeking knowledge of Diane's well-being.

June was contacted, and being a loving and caring person, she chose to enter into communication with Maria. She also accepted a letter for Diane. Though June's intentions were good and loving, her previous preparation for her adoption experience had been nil. She tried to absorb the significance of this latest event in their life. Her friends and family were not supportive of this contact, fearful of negative outcomes.

Eager to learn and quite overwhelmed by her emotions, June met with the social worker. She explained that her daughter had seldom asked adoption-related questions and that she was a model child. Grateful to Maria for allowing her to become a parent by adoption, she felt a desire to share the contact with Diane. When this was done, Diane reacted with excitement and eagerness, wanting to know more about Maria. She went from virtually zero adoption communication to a great deal. She also showed anger about being adopted and expressed a desire to live with Maria. Diane's acting-out behavior lasted for several weeks. This turn of events frightened June and she decided that there would be no more correspondence between Maria and Diane. As a matter of fact, adoption became a fairly taboo subject in that Diane dared not bring it up.

It is vitally important to teach parents about the multidimensional aspects of adoption. This parent, in fact, facilitated some complex communication with her child. At a time when children normally are beginning to express grief, her child was indeed doing this. In fact, the grief process could have been (and probably was) aided by the statements of love and caring from the birthmother. Instead, Diane's clear messages of grief—anger, sadness—were frightening and threatening to her well-intentioned mom. The outcome was that communications, for the time being, were stunted.

Over time, this changed as June worked out her own insecurities. Diane's acting out ceased after a few weeks and her behavior was "back to normal." The outcome was she knew both mothers loved her. One year after the initial sharing, June reports that adoption communication is now at a comfortable level with Diane. She no longer sees any acting out behavior and feels confident about raising the topic with her child.

June continues to correspond with Maria, truly loving her. She shares pictures and news of Diane, acknowledging her

link to Maria. This in itself will serve her well as she deals with
the ongoing process of adoption. Diane demonstrates the flexibility to continue to learn while allowing herself time to work
out future participation.

When and How to Share Difficult Information

Birthparents, being a part of our society at large, will
represent all that our society does—both the glorious, the
problematic, and all the in-between. Questions often arise
regarding what the impact is on the children when the known
information about birthparents is negative. This may include
unstable lifestyles such as multiple marriages and divorces, drug
and alcohol abuse, and problems with the law.

Children derive a sense of self both from their adoptive
families and their birthfamilies. It is vitally important to be
truthful with children in an age-appropriate fashion. No matter how negative the known information is, a focus must be
maintained on the love the birthparents have for the child. As
the child positively internalizes his adoption experience, his
self-concept will be positively impacted. This, in turn, will
allow him to integrate truths about his birthparents, in age-
appropriate dosages, without these truths being internalized
as a reflection of himself. Again, it is important not to fabri-
cate fantasies of a birthparent that does not exist. An approach
that gently conveys that the birthparent has personal problems
will lay the groundwork for future sharing.

Communication becomes the key. From very early ages,
children are keen observers. When personal contact exists, they
absorb that, for example, their birthmother has been married
many times. The stage of development of young children is
such that they tend not to be judgmental. When older, they
will absorb this information with a different level of understanding. How they process this greatly depends on the communication lines they have with their parents.

Ann, whose son Albert is 7½ years old, emphatically
stated that within their family they accentuate the positive
about Albert's birthmother, Kris. Since his birth and adoption,
Kris has married twice, cohabited with a third person, and had
three more children. One of these three children was also

placed for adoption. Ann shares information with Albert in a matter-of-fact, nonjudgmental fashion. Ann's perception is that Kris is still growing up and that they, as Albert's parents, would rather have the contact and knowledge about Kris than not.

Having visits with her allows them to build special bonds that focus on her positive qualities. They feel that their empathy for her is due to the contact they have shared. As the years pass, they love her more and feel optimism that the day will come when her life becomes more stable. Being realists, they know that stability may evade her, nonetheless. They plan to maintain contact—physical and through correspondence— knowing that every family deals with its own trials and tribulations. They have defined Kris as part of their extended family and, as such, contact will continue. They feel comfortable in helping their son process information over time. They focus on messages such as, "You are so special, Albert—Kris made you. Kris is special, too."

Drug and alcohol abuse are certainly other difficult areas to share with children. This is especially true because of genetic predisposition factors and peer pressure on children to participate. Parents may, therefore, fear similar behavior in their children. Parental comfort then becomes crucial in the timing for this sharing. When there is openness that includes physical contact, the child may witness abuse in this area. Communicating about its implications becomes the path to processing its significance. It is important to frame the difficult information in a nonjudgmental way.

The Millers obtained information that their son's birthfather was a hard drug abuser and that he had been in prison many times. His life had been in chaos for a long time and continued to be so, even many years after the adoption. The Millers knew Eddie, nonetheless, cared about their son, Jimmy, now 8½. Over the years this was the message they conveyed to Jimmy. Eddie expressed happiness when he saw Jimmy's pictures and heard about his well-being. The family did not have physical contact with Eddie but felt it was important to stay connected. He was their son's birthfather, and they loved him for that. They knew the day would come when they would share all the known information with Jimmy. They expected that it would cause him some distress and sadness. However, the groundwork of appreciation for who Eddie was would be within him. In addition, they expressed their own acceptance of Eddie. They indicated that they preferred to know the truth, so they could process it themselves over the years.

Guilt and Loyalty Issues in Adopted Children

The conflict of loyalty to both sets of parents is a struggle for children from the preschool years. While they do not yet have a full understanding of adoption in the adult sense, they demonstrate a beginning understanding of the complexities of having two sets of parents.

It is up to the adults in the child's life to convey messages of permission to love the birthparents. Adoptive parents who facilitate contact either through correspondence or physical meetings behaviorally convey this message. It is also important to verbally state that it is perfectly right that a love bond exist between birthparents and child, as well as between child and adoptive parents. This message must be conveyed over the years with consistency. The reason for this is that children often forget over time, and, again, that their understanding varies at different developmental stages.

We have witnessed the internal struggle of children regarding their love for their birthparents. Unburdening them of the guilt for these feelings is vital to their mental health. Some parents give permission by stating their own love for the birthparents. After all, if the parents love them, it surely must be alright for the child to love them, also.

When Amanda was 6 years old she told her adoptive mom that she loved her more than anyone else in the world. Flattered by the intense statement of love, Amanda's mom took the opportunity to let Amanda know how wonderful it felt to be so loved. Then, she added a statement regarding the endless nature of love: "Isn't it wonderful to also love your dad, your sister, grandparents, and birthparents?" The exchange paved the way for future communication.

Who is This?—The Truth Always

An area that some adoptive parents have struggled with is that of how to identify the birthparent. When the child has physical contact, sometimes adoptive parents have expressed a desire to call the birthparent by name without identifying the role of that person. A case in point was Judy. After four years of correspondence with her son's birthmother, Maruja, Judy wanted to finally arrange a meeting including her son. However, she was greatly concerned regarding her son's ability to properly digest the significance of this contact. Her desire therefore, was to introduce Maruja as a friend. After much discussion, this caring but concerned parent agreed it would not be in her son's best interest to misrepresent who Maruja was. Instead, the two mothers met alone and further developed an already loving relationship. The goal became to work toward a future time when Jeremy, their mutual son, could be included.

Scenarios such as this have occurred other times. It is important that adoptive parents facilitate meetings which include the child only when they feel comfortable. This too is a component of entitlement. However, our consistent message is to tell the truth about the identity of the birthparent whenever a meeting takes place.

Birthparents and Correspondence

Birthparents are encouraged to respond to the children with child-appropriate letters including answers and information so often of interest to the child. High on the list of "must include" is a statement regarding the birthparent's feelings for the child and some message regarding how often the child is remembered. Other topics children love to hear about are preferences about food, colors, and sports. They also have a high interest in hearing whether the birthparent has pets and, if so, their names.

Knowing that one is loved and remembered is a vital message to every child, including one with an open adoption. The continuity of the message is important, for children digest and understand different things at different times. Just as we encourage adoptive parents to tell about adoption in an ongoing fashion, so must birthparents tell of their love and caring over the years. Six months or a year is an eternity in the life of a child—he wonders whether his birthparent continues to care. This ongoing message paves the way for adoptees to have trust in the permanence of this love. Trust is an ingredient that so many adoptees have a difficult time with. After experiencing the original loss of the birthparent, trust tends to be a fragile area. What better gift for a birthparent to nurture the well-being of his/her child than to pave the way for skills and experiences that build trust—especially trust in relationships.

When birthparents share information about themselves, the children look for elements of similarity with which to identify. Their sense of self is aided with this knowledge. Katherine, age 10, is a very artistically creative child living with not very artistic adoptive parents. She conveys a tremendous sense of pride knowing that this special gift comes from her birthmother who sews beautifully, does crafts and other manual arts.

It is important to note that children accustomed to receiving correspondence and/or gifts from birthparents are deeply hurt when that birthparent skips a special occasion. This is consistently reported as one of the most significant problems with open adoption. As birthparents go on with their lives and feel content with the knowledge of their child's well-being, they may not realize the impact on the child of decreased or inconsistent contact. We have observed that the behavior the children demonstrate ranges from sadness to anger, even to silence, as one adoptive mother shares:

> Amy, age 12½, hasn't heard from her birthmother in quite a while now, and I think this is puzzling and a little hurtful to Amy. I have explained as best I can why her birthmother might not be able to keep up good contact—but she still has to deal with her feelings. I'm here for her to hug and talk with, and that's all I can do (I should say *we* because my husband is good about listening, too).

The following is shared by Greg's mom. Greg is now 10:

Unfortunately his birthmother's involvement is either
all or none. In a way I think it's easier for him to just get
a simple card once or twice a year than to get very *personal* letters only once in a while. Greg was sad a few
months ago, and we talked about it. He was feeling hurt
because his birthmother had never answered his last letter. He didn't know how to handle his feelings—I just tried
to explain why she may find it hard to write, and this
helps. Also, I reassure him she will never forget him and
always love him. This helps a bit.

When ten-year-old Katherine's birthmother didn't send
a birthday greeting for the second time in a row, Katherine
didn't say much. After a few weeks she decided to write Cindy,
her birthmother, a letter (in fact, she typed the letter herself).
The intrinsic message cannot be mistaken and is very powerful:

Dear Cindy,
    ! How are you? I'am fine How are Mary, Lisa and Susan? I
hope you are find tell Mark hi for me and pleas,' please, tell
Mary a belated happy birthday for me I really feel terrible that
I missed her birthday. Will you please tell me when Lisa and
Susan birthday is so I dont miss them. Cindy I was wondering
since you are not ready to meet me yet would you mind talking on the phone instead?
    I really would appreciate it since Jennifer has talked to Gloria
(her birthmother) and Dinis. Now I feel sory for Jennifer
because Gloria has moved to a different job and Dines has her
phone disconnected and Jennifer,s B-Day is Oct. 15.
    Bye.
                                    Love
                                    Katherine

P.S. I tiped this by myself
    tats why ther are so many mistakes

April 6ᵗʰ, 1987,

Dear Cynde,
It has goten to 25°degres at night.
Last week it snowed in Dallas,Texs.
For Cristmas My dad got me and
Jennifer a puppy. We named it
SnowBall it is a BichonFrisé
How are Felepe and yourself and,
Terry, Cicilia and Jessic?
I'm fine and so is the family.
Love you always,

Love your Dater
Katherine

Katherine's mom felt it was important to help this birth-mother understand Katherine's feelings. Since birthparents are usually not right there witnessing the children's developmental stages and needs, they are somewhat in the dark about these issues. Helping them understand through clear communication becomes the vehicle for building long-term bridges to understanding. Birthparents have a role no adoptive parent can fill. Their message of "I remember you and I love you" is central to the well-being of adopted persons.

Participation Modes

Our experiences with open adoption in this age group include three different participation modes:

1. Children who have had ongoing correspondence, picture and gift exchanges, but no personal meetings.
2. Those who have had ongoing visits with birthparents.
3. Children who originally had closed adoptions, which became modified as in 1 or 2 above.

Let's examine what the impact of these experiences has been for each of these groups.

Children Who Have Correspondence and Gifts Only—No Physical Contact

The philosophy of openness allows for contact whenever the parties involved wish to participate. When we, as professionals, began offering parents options for participation, many parents chose to enter into correspondence with the birthparents. This was done with a great deal of education and counseling—critical ingredients in this process.

The correspondence and picture and gift exchanges between the adults happen at intervals defined by those involved. Typical times for these exchanges have been birthdays and holidays such as Christmas. Some adoptive parents and birthparents are in direct contact with one another, but when professionals act as intermediaries it is important to notify the receiving party. This affords one the opportunity for touching base and being updated regarding what is going on in that person's or family's life. Feedback is requested after the item is received. It is only natural that the sender wishes to know how this gift was received. In this fashion, processing occurs with all parties. It has been invaluable for us, as professionals, to be involved in this capacity, giving us the opportunity to witness the impact of the contact.

The inclusion of children in the correspondence experience evolved naturally. Adoptive parents maintaining contact with birthparents through letters, pictures, and gifts communicated honestly with their children about this. We found that quickly children began to express an interest in participating as well. Comfortable adoptive parents facilitated their inclusion.

Sometimes children who do not know how to write and realize this ask their parents to take their dictation. We have found that children write when the spirit moves them. Usually the letters are brief and tell of activities they are involved with, best friends, pets, teachers names, etc. Sometimes a letter will follow a logical sequence, for example, when a gift has been received. Other times, letters may be written when questions arise for which the adoptive parents have no answer.

We have observed that school-age children who have been receiving letters, cards, and gifts from their birthparents since early childhood, behave in a very laid-back fashion. They are very "matter-of-fact", much like the behavior of natural expectation when grandparents or other loved ones send gifts and cards. The children are pleased, enjoy the moment, and move on.

Katherine

When Katherine was six years old, she wanted to know how long her birthmother was in labor. Her questions regarding this matter became a point of intense fixation. This had to do with the building frustration of not receiving an answer since her mom did not have the information. In an effort to dissipate the mounting feeling, it was decided that Katherine could write to her birthmother and ask for the missing information. With great determination and some help from her mom, Katherine wrote:

Dear Cindy,
How many days were you in labor when you were going to have me? How are your children? How are you?
I'm going to a birthday today. I love your whole family.
Katherine

When the answer arrived, it was dramatic to witness how the information was absorbed and the whole matter became "no big deal." It is amazing to behold such a transformation of emotional energy when an answer becomes available!

Brian and Shannon

Brian, age 9½, had a lot of questions about his birthmother. In typical fashion, he wanted to hear from her so he wrote her a letter. The family had had no previous contact with her. Through their social worker, they received more information than had been given to them at the time of his adoption, including her name, narrative information about her circumstances then and now, etc.

Brian wrote the following letter to his birthmother:

Dear Birthmother,
How are you doing? I'm fine. I like to collect neat rocks, and I want to be an artist. Could you write and send a picture. I'm going on ten. I love you.
Brian

Here is her reply:

Hi,
I thought your letter was nice. Someday I'll send you a picture of myself. Right now here is a picture of Stephen, 8 years old with brown hair and hazel eyes, and Craig, 6 years old with curly brown hair and blue eyes. My hair and eyes are brown. I wear contact lenses and glasses, mostly contact lenses. I'm near-sighted, which means "you can see short distances." I love children and animals. We have a cat named Snowball. I love to take pictures, and in sports I like baseball and tennis. I took one year of art in college. I cannot draw well, but I do like art.

Art is Stephen's favorite subject in school, along with science. If you would like to be an artist, I do wish you the best. Your drawing was very cute. Your picture that you sent was a good one—you are a very handsome boy.

I *love* you very *much* and always will.

Love, Leslie

His parents report that the brief contact that ensued seemed to satisfy him.

His sister, Shannon, also exchanged correspondence with her birthmother at the time Brian did:

Dear Jerri   I had a wonderful day. I'am seven. I like to read. I do good in school. Kerry is my best friend. My brothers name is Brian. I love school. My teachers name is Mrs. Denney. Love Shannon
can I have your picture

will you write to me?

A year and a half later, Sharon, Shannon and Brian's adoptive mother, observes that, although she had some initial apprehensions, she always put herself in her children's place. She feels they have a right to know. A message she asked us to convey is that there was no negative change in the relationship with the children as the result of the correspondence. She also said, with excitement in her voice, that Shannon, now 9½, out of the clear blue had said, "Why does everyone call Jerri my real mother? She's my birthmother." It seems the children at school had been having a conversation about Shannon's adopted status. They were insisting that Sharon was her stepmother and Jerri her "real mother." Shannon emphatically corrected them.

Sharon was clearly moved and went over to Shannon and kissed her and said, "You couldn't say anything nicer to me." Sharon was not trying to convey that Jerri was not real, but in the process of this discussion, she felt very confirmed by her daughter.

Amy

Ann, keenly sensitive to her children, shares how correspondence evolved for their family. When Amy's adoption took place 12½ years ago, closed adoption was the norm. She and her husband shared adoption information with Amy early, using adoption-related books and telling her anecdotes about how their family came to be. However, it amazed and saddened Ann to observe:

> . . . She felt rejected and unloved because of the adoption when she was very young. She was able to share these feelings with me at 3-4 years, but I was unable to allay all of her fears, because she was too young to really understand.
>
> When Amy was in the second grade, she started to have behavior problems related to her feelings about being adopted. Eventually, we got some counseling for her, which helped, and the social worker was able to contact her birthmother and birth grandmother, which really helped. Amy's behavior and feelings about adoption and

herself radically improved. After hearing from her birth-family, she could really feel that they love her and think of her, so she feels "worthy." She has received about three (I think) cards/letters from her birthmother and half brother. These pictures are displayed openly on her dresser, and she has even taken the one of her half brother to school, for friends to see. She is open (and happy) about the idea of some day meeting them, especially her half brother.

Since we have had contact with Amy's birthfamily, I have a greater awareness of her as a separate individual. I don't feel threatened by the birthmother and never have, but I am more *conscious* of Amy being adopted than I used to be. I guess it's never completely out of my mind. Sometimes, I have had fears of rejection relating to Amy as an adult. Sometimes, I'm afraid that when she grows up, she'll just go off with her birthfamily and reject us, but I know these fears are unfounded . . . I don't blame this on open adoption. I really feel more comfortable *knowing* her birthfamily than not. I think it's been basically a *positive* situation for Amy and for me.

On her 13th birthday, Amy received a birthday card from her birthmother and birthgrandparents. When asked how she felt, she said, "It's been a great day—now it's perfect."

From Closed to Openness—Brief Contact

Barbara and Don Clark explored the realities of parenting by becoming foster parents. The first child in their care was a beautiful six-day-old boy. Very quickly their feelings for the child evolved to ones of deep attachment. They decided to pursue his adoption with great determination. To their joy, they received the go-ahead and went through the adoption process. They named their son Bree—which comes from the phrase "Free to Be." His parents believe "he is free to be what and who he wants to be." This philosophy of life led them to an acceptance of the changes in the field of adoption toward increased openness.

When their son was 8½, he was asking questions for which they had no answers. They decided they wanted to respond and to anticipate his needs by opening up their closed adoption. Sensitive to the birthmother's privacy, they used an intermediary in reaching out to Margaret, Bree's birthmother. Initially, Margaret was overjoyed to be contacted. She wrote Barbara, "I am thrilled beyond words to know that Bree is a normal, healthy, beautiful little boy." However, she also stated that at this time in her life, she was not able to participate beyond brief contact. Recently married and still processing her adoption decision, Margaret felt overwhelmed when confronted by Bree's reality. She agreed to accept a letter from Bree and some communication from his parents.

The following are some of the tidbits about Bree which Barbara shared in her letter:

Bree puts potato chips or fries between bread on a sandwich.

He wants to be a comedian like Bill Cosby.

He uses his hands a lot when he talks.

When he's feeling pressure or anxiety, his lips break out with fever blisters.

Margaret reciprocated during a brief correspondence exchange. She wrote Bree and his mom separate letters telling them about herself. She also enclosed two pictures so that Bree could see what she looked like.

In her letter to Barbara, she responded with amazement that she, too, eats sandwiches with potato chips on top of the bread. She stated that her dad had been a hilarious comedian. Like Bree, her hands are also in full motion when she speaks. The fever blister experience is just like that of his birthfather! It was dramatic to see how many areas were identified in this brief exchange that linked Bree to his original family, giving him a greater understanding of his behavioral patterns and whence they came. The genetic influence was dramatically evident in this exchange. Her letter to Bree conveyed warmth, love, and many details about herself:

You know I think you sound like such a special little boy, and I really appreciate the puzzle you made for me. [Bree, on his own, had created a puzzle that said "Thank you for making the right choice—Me!—Bree"]. . . . As you can tell from the photos, I love bright colors—my favorite color is orange. My first favorite thing is eating. My favorite food is Mexican food. . . . I think I will probably wait till you are a little older to write you again. But I do want you to know that I think about you every single day, and I have always known you are a VERY SPECIAL LITTLE BOY. And you will always have a special place in my heart.

> *I love you,*
> *Margaret*

When Bree received his letter, he said, "I just think this is really neat." His mother reports that he stared and stared at the letter and pictures. Bree has expressed a desire to meet Margaret. His parents used the opportunity to help Bree understand his birthmother's feelings and apprehensions. They will continue to do this over time, but, for now, Bree demonstrates a comfort level with the knowledge about his birthmother. They feel they have done their part to open the door. The next step is hers.

Approaching Birthfathers

There are many birthfathers in our society who have been excluded from adoption involvement through personal choice or because of the process, which typically focuses on the birthmother. A great deal of mystery and secrecy surrounds the role of birthfathers—often to a greater degree than that of birthmothers. We must continue to strive for a greater involvement on the part of birthfathers, for they, after all, constitute 50% of the child's heritage. The reality is that there are many caring birthfathers who, by themselves, deal with the separation-by-adoption. The children need to know about them, too. When possible, contact benefits all parties, akin to the contact with the birthmother.

The Clarks recognized the important role of their son's birthfather and took steps to locate him, too. They had planned to do this even if Margaret (birthmother) had agreed to ongoing contact. They were committed to laying the groundwork for a relationship that would endure over time. Shortly before Bree's 10th birthday, an intermediary was again used to contact Bill, his birthfather. At first Bill was somewhat surprised, asking for time to process the significance of this event. He did not understand how communication with Bree would benefit the child or himself. Materials were dispatched so that he, too, could learn more about the effects of adoption on all three parties. Within a short time, communication began to take place through correspondence and by telephone.

The following is an excerpt of Bill's letter to Bree's parents:

> I want to thank you for your patience and the manner in which you contacted me. I have harbored years of frustration and guilt over what has been a major event in my life. Your sincere and delicate approach helped me overcome these negative feelings and put the entire matter in perspective. . . . Thank you for helping me understand and deal with what has been a very difficult time in my life. Just knowing Bree is alive, healthy, and happy has been a tremendous relief.

Regarding the adoption decision, he says: " . . . it was not a matter of making the right or wrong decision for ourselves, but rather making the best decision for Bree."

Bill also wrote Bree a letter for his 10th birthday. He gave him details of his talents, interests, and a flavor of his growing-up years. The letter was upbeat and warm. The content was just what Bree wanted to hear. It validated so many of his attributes and interests, thus providing him with a powerful connection.

Bill included in his letter that much needed answer to "Why adoption?":

> We loved you very much, but decided we could not give you the home and parenting that you deserved. We wanted you to have a home with two parents who care for you and love each other. . . . Our decision was very difficult, because separately we both loved you very much and did not want to give up a part of ourselves. I am very

grateful that we were able to find you the wonderful parents that you now have. Someday I hope you will understand. . . . I think about you often. . . . I care for you very much. . . .

Bree is particularly fortunate in that he has confirmation of love and caring from both birthparents. It is vital to recognize that adopted children need this from both parties. As sensitive adoptive parents facilitate contacts such as this, more and more birthparents will grow to understand how truly vital they are in their children's lives.

Communication: Dealing With Grief

Sally had written to her son David's birthmother only a few times during David's early years. This was in part due to the fact that the adoption began as a closed one. As changes in practice occurred, Sally felt comfortable writing the birthmother a few times. David was not a part of this exchange. Sally kept up with the new learning taking place in the field of adoption. She watched her child go through many developmental stages. She noted that he was a very private child when it came to the sharing of emotions.

She had absorbed with interest the grief other children expressed about being adopted. David had not demonstrated anything that seemed to be a part of the grief process. She was aware that children go through stages within their own time frames.

All of a sudden the dam broke. In an emotional exchange when David was 8, he expressed his innermost need to know about his birthparents and to gain answers to a multitude of questions. Sally validated her child, letting him know that she would make every effort to obtain the knowledge that he needed. Sally reflects:

When David was four years old, I wrote Margie (his birthmother) for the first time in order to let her know about him. I had attended lectures periodically about adoption. The one overall theme that I learned was that birthmothers always think about their child, especially during holidays or at birthdays. So I wrote in order to let her know he was doing well.

The years passed. David, now 8, started asking about his birthmother indirectly by remarking that his friend Keith looked like his mother. My husband and I quickly realized that David was curious about his identity. I asked him if he had been wondering about his birthparents. He quickly denied his interest. However, I remained persistent and he soon opened up his thoughts and began to explain his desire to know more about his birthmother. He asked why she had given him up. I told him that she loved him very much but wanted him to have opportunities and things she could not afford. David's response to that comment was, "But, Mom, she could have gotten a job!"

It became clear to me that he was grieving strongly and angry that his birthmother had given him up. What was most clear to me, however, was the fact that, although I had intellectually understood some issues in adoption, I had in only eight years forgotten to keep in mind one of the most crucial segments of my son's existence. I, like an ostrich with its head in the sand, had let myself forget about the importance of my son's birthmother.

That night, David's questions and comments were overflowing, and he was weeping as he told me, "You just don't know how tough it is not to know your birthmother." We sat together in the big black recliner in the living room as I read him the sketch of his birthparents, grandparents, and great grandparents. He was so delighted to know that his grandfather was musical and played the guitar, because he, too, at that time was taking guitar lessons. He listened and asked for me to reread the page again. When we finished, I asked him if he would like to write to his birthmother and have the social worker at the agency send the letter to her, he jumped at the chance. I questioned him, "What would happen if she did not answer your letter?" to which he responded, "That will be very sad."

It was already 10:00 P.M., and we were both emotionally exhausted. Nonetheless, that very night he dictated the following letter:

Dear Birthmother and Birthfather:

Will you please take a picture of each of you if my birthfather is there. What are your names? I am eight years old. I am four feet tall. I wear a size three large in shoes, and a ten regular in clothes.

I have a dog. He is 10 months old. He got adopted by us. He was a stray dog that was usually around our school. His name is Lucky.

I wish that you were here.

From,
David

Please write me.

Contact was made with Margie. She had had her own struggles regarding her decision for adoption. She quickly grasped the opportunity to respond to David and wrote him a child-appropriate letter, including pictures of herself and the birthfather. The following are excerpts from Margie's letter:

I was very excited when I was told that you were interested in knowing more about me and your birthfather. I was even more excited when I found out you were writing a letter for me . . . I received your pictures, and I can't begin to explain how much they mean to me. I enjoy reading, fishing, listening to music . . . My favorite foods are anything with cheese, especially enchiladas, cheeseburgers, and pizza . . . I want you to know that I have not forgotten you. I think about you a lot. I have always wanted to write you, but sometimes it's very hard to explain to someone how you feel . . . I do love you very much. I wanted you to have the best in life. . . .

This profound experience allowed this child to work through the grief he was experiencing. It did not deny or belittle his feelings but rather acknowledged that as part of the healing process, the birthmother and adoptive parents had significant roles to play. He was validated, supported and responded to. Sally continues:

> The following January, I reminded David that Margie's birthday was coming up and asked him if he wanted to send her a birthday card. I still recall this young nine-year-old meeting me at the check-out line at the grocery store delighted as he held a special birthday card which he had carefully chosen for his birthmother.

DEAr MArGiE.
iwiSh yOU A .HAPpy BirTh dAy.
iLiKEd you r LETTr.
FroM DAViD

This marked the beginning of correspondence between David and Margie. The letters have become more casual in nature. There seems to be the comfortable awareness that now that the door is open they will all get to know each other better. David writes:

Dear Margie,

I wish I could see you in person someday on your birthday.

I'm enjoying going to a new school this year, and I'm getting mostly A's on my report cards.

I really like computers, bikes, skate boards, roller skates, and especially you.

Love,
David

Sally acknowledges that her comfort with openness has increased over time, remembering that it all began as a closed adoption:

> I must admit that, while I wanted some degree of openness, I did not want to reveal too much that might leave me vulnerable. . . . Now, I have progressed to an entirely different level. I feel David is part of a cycle of life that is his own to learn about. There is, indeed, an

adoption triangle. I cannot wish it away, nor do I want to anymore. I was beginning to get ready to meet his birthmother. I was starting to feel that perhaps David could indeed meet her, too.

Shortly before David's eleventh birthday, Sally asked to meet Margie face to face:

> We met at the agency for about three and a half hours. The meeting was so incredible. Margie shared all the feelings and events that surrounded David's birth, his birthfather, her family. She questioned me about David, our family's response to an adopted child, and expressed her interest and readiness to meet him face to face. She sent another letter and pictures of her husband and all her immediate family members. Through discussion and pictures, we were beginning to gain a sense of hereditary personality traits and temperament, as well as physical similarities.

David, age 11, expressed the desire to meet Margie, noting "I have always wanted to meet her." Margie, too, was ready. Sally conveyed, through her social worker, a readiness to have David meet with his birthmother. When David was presented with this, he lit up and enthusiastically endorsed the plan. All the principals had been validated and allowed to evolve at their own rates.

The groundwork, in the form of correspondence, assisted in the next stage of getting acquainted. David dictated a letter to his mom for Margie, his birthmother. With obvious delight, he said, "This is weird—telling my mother to write to my mother! "

The day finally came for David and Margie to meet face-to-face. Sally shares her feelings about that long-anticipated moment, a visit in their home:

> We had borrowed a video camera to record the special moments. When the bell rang, David answered the door and called to me, "Mom, it's for you." We all came into the living room, Margie carrying a photo album and

David armed with the video camera. It was obvious we were all nervous and emotional. Margie commented on David's looks, remarking how he looked like her sister and brother. David was quiet and took a lot of footage with the video camera, being able to freely stare at Margie.

The visit lasted 1½ hours. When I suggested that David take Margie into his bedroom and playroom, he tugged at my arm and demanded, "You come, too." It was then that I realized that the 'competition' that I had feared all these years was unwarranted. I was, indeed, David's Mom, and Margie was someone important, someone he had wanted to see and know, yet he felt safe with me.

In fact, later when I remarked, "David, some people would think that your birthmother visiting is crazy on our part because she might want you back," he quickly replied, "Yeah, *right*, Mom—Margie comes in and says 'OK, David, come live with me'—GET REAL." It was evident the he knew where his Home was and wanted no changes.

I feel a great sense of having done the right thing. Our daily lives will probably not change that much, but the internal impact has already been far-reaching for all of us.

Our experience has been that these youngsters get a clearer sense of self, absorbing the realities of their birth families. They also are able to integrate the role of the birthparents, while affirming the parents who are raising them. Parents who choose to respond to the expressed need of their child only bond more tightly with them, as mentioned before regarding adoption communication in the family.

Each level of communication allows fixations on the part of children to dissipate. The typical pattern leads to the taking of contact and knowledge in stride. This is akin to how most of us absorb and integrate our own families of origin—sometimes being so matter-of-fact that it gets taken for granted. It's that ease of relationships that is the norm. In adoptions which have moved from closed to open, that "norm" must be reestablished over time because of the duration of the break in contact.

From Closed to Open—Another Experience

Stacy Speedlin, age 9, had expressed an intense desire to have contact with her birthparents. Her responsive parents understood that a fixation was taking place and felt the need to mobilize contact, first through correspondence. This had been a closed adoption with no contact for the preceding nine years. Phylis and Dick, her parents, stated that Stacy felt she was not OK:

> Since Stacy has very dark hair with dark skin, she convinced herself that this was why she was "given away." These were her own words. In her mind, her birthmother became blond with light skin.

Stacy's parents sought help through their agency, but the professionals who had had contact with Stacy's birthmother were reluctant. They told Phylis that they felt that "Stacy's birthmother was too emotional to handle contact." Phylis recalls, "That made wanting to open Stacy's adoption very difficult. What if we were wrong? However, Stacy's self-concept was dramatically worsening. We decided to approach her birthmother through a professional intermediary. At first, Stacy's birthmother was thrilled but, then, scared. She wanted to keep the relationship closed. We respected her wishes."

They then decided to reach out to Stacy's birthfather, Ali. He was immediately found. He later told the family that he had planned to stay in the same house and city until Stacy found him. Over a period of a few months, the adults wrote one another, getting acquainted and building trust. Many emotions were shared in this exchange. It was evident that the ultimate goal was a relationship including physical contact.

The process included individual counseling sessions of preparation with the birthparent and the adoptive parents. These sessions covered a wide array of adoption-related issues. The adoptive parents were extremely sophisticated in their knowledge and understanding regarding adoption (Phylis is the co-author of *Dear Birthmother*). They also were highly sensitive to their daughter's needs.

The sessions with the birthfather were ones that covered the whole gamut of the last nine years and his hopes for the future now that the opportunity for contact existed. The social worker and Ali went back in time, examining the circumstances regarding his daughter's birth and adoption, his feelings for his daughter then and now, his relationship with the birthmother and his coping mechanisms during the years of no knowledge about his child. This birthfather cared deeply for his child and the years of grieving finally were becoming a time of healing as he was able to be included in her life.

It became clear that there was a great affinity and a shared love among these adults. Phylis, Dick, and Ali agreed that a meeting including Stacy was the next step. Not wanting to overlook appropriate evaluation regarding Stacy's readiness, they arranged a session with an adoption-experienced play therapist. They received the confirming go-ahead. Stacy demonstrated a healthy readiness and a need (normal for an adopted person) to meet her birthfather.

The Meeting

It must be underlined that continued preparation, support, and processing are vitally important ingredients that we offer as professionals. There have been adoptive families and birthparents who have chosen to navigate their relationships on their own. Their right to self-determination must be respected. However, for those who include us, we are able to offer a broad spectrum of experience that is valuable as we offer support over the years.

When a meeting occurs, whether it includes children or not, it is essential that some time be devoted on the day of the meeting to discuss what the expectations, fantasies, concerns, etc. may be. This is, again, done individually with the adoptive family and with the birthparent(s). At the end, processing regarding content and feelings occurs individually with the participants—the adoptive family as a unit and the birthparents separately.

Before the meeting, typically, everyone is nervous and

anxious. They worry about whether they will like each other, what they will say, their appearance, and so on. The excitement level is also high. It is a sight to behold—a competent, capable adult become a bundle of nerves. Our role is to assuage the fears and facilitate comfort as this face-to-face contact is about to take place.

In contrast to meetings involving infants and preschoolers, when a school-age child is involved, he participates in all aspects of these steps of preparation with his parents. It is of utmost importance to give the child the freedom to decide whether he wishes to embrace or kiss the birthparent upon greeting or parting. Topics of discussion are not limited but permission is given for the child to ask questions of his choice. During the meeting time we stay with the participants for as long as seems appropriate. When school-age children are involved, we typically participate during most or all of the meeting. This is for the purpose of observing what the child's comfort level is and to intervene if it seems necessary. We also are one more support source for the child.

Stacy Meets Ali

School-age children, especially those in the younger ranges, don't have a full understanding about adoption. Therefore we emphasize beforehand that after the meeting, they will go home with their parents. We make a concerted effort to walk them through the meeting so that we address as many unspoken fears as we can. The fear that permanence might be in jeopardy is addressed as a high priority.

When Stacy met Ali, her parents sat with her, offering her the support she obviously needed. Especially at a first meeting it is important to stay with the child unless the child requests some time alone with the birthparent or is so obviously at ease that the absence of the adoptive parents is not distressing. We strive to maintain a secure atmosphere for the child throughout.

The day of the meeting with Ali, Stacy was excited and very nervous. Would he like her? Did she look OK? What would she say? Stacy's way of handling her nervous feelings was to crack joke after joke. Ali absorbed her presence with his eyes and his soul, asking no questions, only remarking in response to her statements. It was obviously an intense moment for everyone. The meeting lasted about an hour. This was to be the first of many visits.

The Aftermath

As with any relationship, time increases the comfort level. Phylis reflects:

> Subsequent to the first meeting, Stacy met Ali in "safe" places on her birthday and Christmas. In the three years that followed, meetings and/or phone calls became spontaneous. As these meetings became more comfortable, Stacy's self-concept improved. She stopped looking for reasons that she was "bad" or "ugly" to explain her placement.
>
> Ali sent me a beautiful flower arrangement the first Mother's Day after that first meeting. The note simply said, "Thank you for being Stacy's Mom." What a powerful way to confirm our family unit.
>
> Sometime later Stacy's birthmother decided to meet Stacy. She was more nervous than Stacy. She wanted to run out of the room because she was sure Stacy wouldn't like her.
>
> Since then she has contacted Stacy only through short letters. She maintains the contact she feels is safe. Stacy loves contact especially since her relationship with Ali and Ami (her birthsister) is so consistent and "accepted" now.

When One Child Has Openness and the Other Doesn't

We often have distraught adoptive parents seeking guidance when one child has some level of openness and the other has less or none at all. Sometimes they feel it is in the best interest of their family to not participate in contact. This consideration comes into play out of concern for the child who has less openness available. It is difficult for parents to witness their child's envy and sadness.

Realizing that this is a difficult situation, we point out that life brings about many inequities and that the balance may someday shift. Is it right to cut off a potential source of good for one child in order to protect the other child? These are difficult questions for parents to weigh. Our recommendation is that parents use the contact opportunity for one child to assist the other child. We must use whatever tools we have at our disposal to assist the children in dealing with this complex experience.

In addition, we have found that birthparents are very sensitive to the sibling of their child. They tend to include these children in telephone conversations and correspondence, send thoughtful gifts to both children, and generally behave as extended family would towards the entire family.

Two stories highlight what we call the unequal birthparent involvement. For the better part of nine years Katherine received letters, cards, and occasional gifts from her birthmother. It was difficult for her younger sister, Jennifer, to witness this because Jennifer's birthmother, Gloria, had chosen to disengage from contact shortly after the adoption took place. Support was provided to Jennifer via assurances that someday contact would likely occur. Additionally the statements of love from Katherine's and other birthmothers were used to vicariously help Jennifer experience another birthparent's love. It still was difficult but eased by the first letter Gloria wrote at the time of her birth, which included a picture of older siblings being raised by Gloria.

When Jennifer was almost 7 her birthmother, Gloria, suddenly contacted the agency seeking knowledge of Jennifer's well-being. Seven years of waiting and hoping for contact came to resolution when this happened. A letter covering Jennifer's first seven years was promptly dispatched along with unmailed "letters" that Jennifer had written Gloria during her preschool years. The latter had not been sent previously because no current address had ever been located. In addition, about 200 pictures highlighting Jennifer's growth and development were finally sent to Gloria. Favorite duplicates had been put to one side all these years in hopes that someday Gloria would finally be able to behold this magnificent little girl. Last but not least, Jennifer's hand prints, carefully outlined for the last many years, were sent as a gesture of sharing her growth from infancy.

Jennifer received her first letter from Gloria on her seventh birthday along with the presents from her family. She smiled a lot but otherwise did not verbalize a great deal of emotion. Later that day, when asked how she felt when she saw the letter, she stated that she was happy and that she felt like crying. It was obvious the emotion had been positive and intense. This contact had a tremendous impact on the family as Jennifer received the concrete evidence that, in fact, Gloria still loved her and always had.

Several months later it was decided that a telephone call was to be the next step since Gloria lives in California and Jennifer in Texas. Katherine was invited to participate in this. Without hesitation she said she too wanted to talk with Gloria. The conversation was taped so that Gloria's words and voice would be available to Jennifer whenever she chose to hear the tape.

Segments of the conversation (which includes common themes, such as ongoing love, similarities, etc.) have been transcribed to convey themes helpful to children:

I love you so much. I would like to meet you someday.

Are you a good girl?

I like your pictures—you look beautiful.

You love your mommy? Yes [Jennifer's answer]. Good!

You look just like Ernie, your brother.

He's very thin like you.

Don't worry about being small—I'm small. I'm 5 feet.

Be a good girl.

Send me all the pictures you want.

You just made my day. Thank you.

I love you guys—hugs and kisses!

Significant in this exchange was Katherine's ambivalence. Now a shift had occurred and Jennifer had more direct contact than she had. Katherine had been hungering for telephone and physical contact for many years. She expressed her vicarious absorption of Gloria by saying with emotion—"She said she loved me." This was followed by later acknowledged jealousy when she said "Gloria has an ugly voice."

When Jennifer walked up and down the halls of her home hearing Gloria's tape, luxuriating in the message of love, Katherine kept a low profile. The imbalance was painful for her and her parents. However, it was important that Jennifer too receive her confirmation of self-worth through Gloria's continued love.

The outcome of the contact was that Jennifer went through a dramatic shift in her sense of security. Where before she demonstrated a marked insecurity and sadness, she now displays a sense of well-being; she smiles more fully. She received from Gloria that which her nurturing parents could not provide her: a confirmation of love and caring from her first mother.

So the balance shifted for Katherine and Jennifer. In each case, the greater degree of contact was used for both children—one with direct benefit and one using it vicariously—looking toward the day when the balance would once again shift.

The shift came at Christmastime when Katherine joyfully received handmade clothing items from Cindy. She nearly burst with excitement as she beheld a T-shirt dress which fit to a tee with a matching bow. Additionally, a beautifully decorated T-shirt with her name was neatly tucked under the dress. By now, there had been a time span of many months without contact with Gloria. She had changed jobs and had not given the new telephone number to Jennifer's family. Jennifer's eighth birthday had come and gone with silence on Gloria's part. Jennifer did not demonstrate distress, still buoyed by the previous contacts.

Sensitive to a probable emotional reaction from Jennifer, her mom took her aside and told her of Katherine's gifts. Jennifer sobbed at her own current lack of contact and gifts. Most of all, she lamented that she didn't even have a promised picture of Gloria.

To witness Jennifer's intense grief was difficult for her family. Many tears were shared and comfort attempted. Katherine in an unusual gesture, took Jennifer on her lap and lovingly told her that she knew Gloria loved her very much and that she was sorry Gloria hadn't sent a gift or a picture. As a matter-of-fact, she promised to ask Cindy to make something for Jennifer. She went on to tell her that she, Katherine, felt terrible when Jennifer had the opportunity to talk with Gloria on the telephone and she had never been able to hear Cindy's voice on the phone.

In spite of the pain shared by this family, there was an emotional bridge traveled in the area of love among its members and connection with birthparents. Honest and tender communication became an important outcome. Again, this family handled the shift in balance by not curtailing contact with the birthparent which benefited the child. Support was provided to the child who, at this time, needed it.

Another Family Allows for Imbalance

Deanna and Ronnie had been corresponding with Brooke's (age 7) birthmother since Brooke was an infant. Bryan, their 11-year-old son, had no contact with his birthmother. This was his birthmother's choice. She had consistently asked that no one contact her. She indicated that when she felt ready she would come forward to receive letters being saved for her in the file.

Bryan's parents responded lovingly to his questions and needs, assuaging his obvious disappointment and pain at not having contact with his birthmother. They had written to the birthmother requesting ongoing correspondence for Bryan, but she was not comfortable participating. Patti, Brooke's birthmother, always included Bryan in her letters and sent Christmas gifts for both children. Again, the vicarious experience was used.

At age 7, Brooke was pressing for a meeting with Patti. She had corresponded with her over time and had sent pictures during the preschool years. Now, she expressed a deep desire to see Patti in the flesh, as her mother relates:

Right before Brooke's eighth birthday, she said she would like to meet her birthmom. Just out of the blue, she said that. Just as off-the-cuff as "What's for supper?" We talked about her thoughts and feelings and off she went to play. I decided not to act immediately and to wait for her to bring it up again. About two months passed when she asked me if I had contacted the agency to make arrangements to meet her birthmom. I told her I had waited for her to be sure that's what she really wanted. She emphatically said, "Yes." So I got the wheels rolling.

Deanna admitted that years before she would not have been ready for this possibility. However, the years of correspondence had built up a trust in the relationship they shared with Patti and close attention was paid to Brooke's request. When approached, Patti was delighted that a meeting was to be arranged if she wished it. She definitely did. Patti herself identified a need to meet personally with a professional to process her many emotions and to have some insight into how these meetings had gone before with other school-age children.

Among the important areas covered were the typical behavior of children in this age group; her feelings when Brooke called her adoptive mother "Mommy"—a name she, Patti, would not be called by this, her firstborn; and natural feelings of sadness when it was time to part again. Patti was sensitized to Bryan's closed adoption and his frustrated needs. She had always included him and this time would be no different.

Brooke and her family also met for a preparation session to cover their expectations, fantasies, questions, etc. Brian was included in this family session too, being given the opportunity to express his yearning. Brooke indicated that she wanted to see what Patti looked like in person and she wanted to know what she was like. Brooke was nervous and excited.

With children, it is important to schedule the preparatory session close to the day of the meeting so as to not overly prolong the anxiety level. This also helps children remember the topics covered, so as to better retrieve that which may be helpful.

The meeting took place two days later in Corpus Christi, where Patti lives. After initial nervousness, both children relaxed and animatedly participated in the group conversation. Brooke did not ask adoption-related questions, but rather absorbed Patti's presence. She demonstrated tremendous comfort in her company and even asked to travel in her car to the restaurant where they had lunch. Both sets of parents were at ease with this travel arrangement.

The following is Deanna's account of how this meeting impacted on Brooke and her family:

> I felt like I was going to see a sister I hadn't seen in a long time. Brooke was filled with curiosity and excitement. Our meeting was incredibly positive with not enough time—endless conversation. Even the social worker asked if we had ever met before because our communication was so enjoyable. Why shouldn't it be—we are family! I cannot find the words to express the joy I felt being able to physically hug the woman who gave my daughter life and to tell her how I felt about her. And to share the bond I have with her through the life of this precious child we share. And the bond of pain—hers for knowing she wasn't ready to be a parent and that adoption was necessary; and my pain of not being able to birth this child. But we can share the joy of this child. This child's life makes us complete.
>
> Brooke said it as completely as I ever could. After a few days had passed since our first visit with her birthmother, I asked her how she felt about the visit—happy, sad, lonesome to see them again, etc? And, with the most beautiful expression of joy and peace, she replied, "Everything is OK, momma; I *KNOW* now."

Patti shares her perspective after meeting Brooke and her family in a letter to the social worker:

> Thank you so much for arranging our meeting! It went great! At first, I was a little nervous, but Brooke took

care of that. She warmed up real fast! She talked a lot (more than I expected) and was so well-behaved. We all decided to have lunch together and Brooke asked Deanna, "Do you think some people have room in their car for Brian and me?" She's so cute! I didn't get to tell her everything I wanted to. She didn't really have any questions. Maybe I didn't encourage her to ask questions like I should have. We all felt real good about having direct contact with each other.

Patti further shares her feelings in a letter to the family:

I feel such peace having met you all and knowing that Brooke has such a loving family. And that she doesn't seem to have any ill feelings toward me. I'm thankful that you were open with her about adoption. Maybe she'll understand that grown-ups can be shy, too. I just wanted to tell her that I love her and am proud of her.

I don't want you to feel threatened for Brooke. I would never do anything to hurt that precious little girl, especially to try to take her from a family that I know means so much to her. And I can see that you have raised her well.

When Communication Readiness is not Mutual

Much insight has been gained over the years pertaining to communication desires of one party when there is hesitation on the part of the other. We will examine here the issues affecting birthparent hesitation or non-participation.

When adoptive parents go through a good educational foundation regarding adoption, they are usually more likely to want openness. With education comes understanding and a desire for contact over the years. As their sensitivity to adoption increases, their desire to include the birthmother also increases. Unfortunately, adoptive parents and birthparents are not always at the same point of comfort in dealing with the myriad adoption issues. Sometimes birthparents are fearful of even receiving correspondence about their child, thinking it will cause emotional havoc to witness the reality of the child.

We have found that for those who allow themselves to confront their fears and emotions, that the contact proves to be cathartic and confirming of their decision. The processing opportunity when dealing with an experienced professional is invaluable. Time and time again those reluctant birthparents have reported how glad they are that they chose to participate in spite of their fears.

Let's examine what the fears entail. Birthparents report that when emotionally dealing with their adoption decision, they sometimes remain in a state of numbness—intertwined with grief and guilt. They often wonder if their decision was a good one, whether the adoptive parents speak well of them to the child, and whether the child hates them for the adoption choice. When no contact is available, birthparents are more likely to fixate on these issues, attacking their self-esteem and not progressing in the working through of the separation from their child.

When contact becomes available, they fear that hearing about the child will make their journey more difficult and feed feelings of regret. Rather than risk this, they choose no contact. Birthparents who consider the latter but choose to risk consistently report that contact assists them in having affirmation for their decision. It is also helpful in redefining their relationship to their child as the birthparent, while acknowledging the adoptive parents as the nurturing parents. Contact, in fact, affirms all roles in the adoption triangle.

When Jason was 6 years old, his mom, Evelyn, requested that their closed adoption change to one embodying contact. His birthmother, Shirley, was notified of this. Shirley expressed hesitation, fearing the painful impact upon her psyche. She loved Jason deeply and feared the wounds that might further develop within her because of contact. Being a candid person, willing to take risks, Shirley responded positively to Evelyn. She would accept correspondence and pictures and allow herself to feel their effects.

At first, she reported a mixture of sadness and joy. Hearing about Jason brought her healing—he was well and obviously loved. The sadness had to do with the fact that she was not part of his life as a parent. She once again, on a conscious level, had to deal with this. To her surprise, she found that with every contact, she felt better about the adoption decision and its rightness. Each contact provided her with an increasing sense of well-being. Shirley and Evelyn reached a point of mutual comfort and met in person. They now live in different states and contact through correspondence occurs several times a year. After four years of contact, Shirley shares:

> I wish I had even more contact. I had felt so much guilt and now that is gone. Knowing Jason is in good hands, seeing how he looks and how he's being brought up makes me know I made the right decision. . . . Even when I didn't want to have contact, I felt that I should and that it was the right thing to do. I'd like to tell other birthmothers not to be afraid and not to feel guilt. Contact will make them feel better.

☐ 6 ☐

THE SCHOOL-AGE CHILD
PART II

Ongoing Visitation—Open from the Start

Families who opted for ongoing visitation from the beginning now have children who are school age. Consistently their message has been that they would not trade this experience for anything. These children are comfortably integrating the birthparents as special persons in their lives. These families differ from the ones who went from closed to open only in that they chose direct contact immediately. They didn't feel the need to build up a relationship—they already felt its presence when the adoption took place.

Brett

Jan and Jerry Gass adopted their son, Brett, eight years ago. They chose ongoing visitation. While Lillian (Brett's birthmother) lived in Texas, they would see her three to four times a year. When the visits took place in San Antonio, where the Gass family resides, Lillian was their houseguest. As such, Jan reports that the relationship that has evolved is one embodying natural behavior and a deep friendship. These visits have always been lighthearted and fun.

Lillian now lives in a different state. Periodically, Brett asks to speak with her on the phone. Sometimes he asks if vacation will include a side trip to Lillian's. Jan feels that the contact has helped Brett understand adoption. As he gets older, she foresees sending him by himself to visit Lillian. The bond and the trust are there for all of them.

Brett comments:

> When Lillian moved I was sad because I don't get
> to see her as often . . . She sent pictures of my two
> brothers and they are *really, really* good pictures. I feel
> good knowing about them.

Haley

Robbie and Michael Archer also opted for ongoing contact, meeting with their daughter Haley's birthparents before
her birth. Immediately following the adoption, the birthparents withdrew from contact. Before Haley was two, her parents initiated efforts to reestablish contact. At first the
birthparents, Joan and Richard, were reluctant because of all
the emotions they felt. However, shortly thereafter they came
forward.

The frequency of contact is determined by those
involved. Robbie states that they see Joan and Richard at least
twice a year. Haley is now 7 years old and shows all the signs
of positive adjustment. She knows that her birthparents are
now married and have a son, her brother. Her parents were
pleased to see her matter-of-fact comfort as she shared news
of her brother with her adoptive grandfather. Her very comfortable manner has reinforced the process. Sometimes she
expresses the wish that she could see them more often, as her
younger sister does with her birthmother. The frequency has
been largely determined by her birthparents' pacing and everyone's respect of boundaries. Robbie realized that Haley had
unspoken fantasies about her birthparents, especially because
they usually only see each other on special occasions. She
wished that Haley could see Joan and Richard more frequently
so that the fantasies could be worked through.

As a result, Robbie encouraged Haley's birthparents to
invite Haley to their home by herself. Recently Haley spent the
day with her birthparents and her full brother. Haley demonstrated a well-being about this visit. Robbie felt this marked
the beginning of a more casual interaction among them. She
wants her daughter to know her birthparents' love at close
hand. She also feels it is important to respond to Haley's

expressed desire to see her birthparents more frequently. Robbie and Michael do not want Haley to expend energy fantasizing or yearning. They want her to develop a special relationship with her birthparents, and they do not feel threatened by this relationship which they hope will continue to develop. They strongly feel this will only benefit Haley and their family as a whole. They, too, have a special relationship with her birthparents; a friendship that is bonded by similar values and interests.

The trust Robbie and Michael demonstrate as they allow Joan and Richard to be with Haley has grown as the relationship evolved. They know Joan and Richard would never do anything to hurt Haley or the permanence of Haley in their family. Their common goal is to strive for Haley's well-being.

It is not uncommon for fantasies to be part of the adoption experience. Fortunately, the open-adoption process allows for fantasies to be replaced by reality. Robbie and Michael are committed to helping Haley through her stages, including those pertaining to the grief associated with adoption. One must bear in mind that openness doesn't eliminate grief, but it allows for that grief to be confronted and worked through with the involvement and support of all the principals. Another dimension of the ongoing contact is the flexibility within this process to add and change relationships over time. Sometimes, because of readiness factors, the birthfamily doesn't engage in contact immediately.

Neil

Loo and Mel Thaler attended workshops regarding adoption well before they became adoptive parents. They had observed relatives' experiences with closed adoption and decided that method was not for them. When they adopted Neil eight years ago, they felt committed to ongoing contact with Neil's birthparents. Lori, his birthmother, enthusiastically participated in visitation, which was comfortable to all. Neil's birthfather, Steve, however, had not yet reached the point of publicly acknowledging his son. It took him approximately a year to come forward and enter into contact with the Thalers. He then accepted correspondence and a visit. It was a joyful gathering. Pictures were taken recording this memorable event. Even as this visit was taking place, Steve had not yet acknowledged to his family that he had fathered this child. Tragically, several weeks later, Steve was killed in a violent car crash. Heartbroken, his parents began the difficult task of going through his belongings. They discovered pictures and letters verifying Neil's existence. Their grief was compounded now that they had to deal not only with the death of their son, but also the loss of Neil through adoption. Fortunately, through the process of healing, they were able to face both major events. When Neil was 4 years old, a meeting was arranged so they could meet Neil and his parents.

The years have passed and contact has continued with both sides of the birthfamily. The Thalers report that Neil continues to process open adoption very well. Loo states, "To Neil it [his adoption] is neither something to be ashamed of nor something to be overly proud of—it is just something that is."

We must recognize that even the children who have had visitation from the beginning need to have communication within the family about what all of this means. It must not be assumed that because of the contact that the child easily processes its significance. Each contact is an opportunity for clarification and elaboration.

Like other children in their situation, Neil, Brett, and Haley are digesting their total family in gradual dosages. Their parents agree with Loo Thaler when she says that they "feel no threat of parental or family substitution. *We have experienced no problems.*" In fact, for those separated by distance, often the statement is that they wish they could see each other more frequently. There is a mutual feeling of being family with a unity of purpose, having at its center the well-being of the children.

The Children of Open Adoption Teach Others

The Albrechts met Katherine on placement day. After correspondence for the first 18 months, they met again. Since then, they have participated in regular visitation and phone calls. Emily, now 6½, decided she wanted to take a picture of her birthmother and birthgrandmother to "Show and Tell" at school. Her mother, Judy, prepared Emily for her classmates' possible questions.

Judy shares the questions they discussed and Emily's answers:

Question: Why were you placed for adoption?

Answer: Because my birthmother wanted me to have a father, as well. And because she was a baby herself.

Question: Did that mean she didn't love you?

Answer: No, she loves me very much.

Question: Does that mean she threw you away?

Answer: No, she made a plan for me to be parented.

As we witness Emily's answers, it is obvious that this area had been discussed previously. She displayed total comfort and a grasp of what she was saying. Judy observed that for Emily to share her adoption with her classmates was an indicator of Emily's state of comfort with adoption. It also gave a gauge of Emily's self esteem. Adoption was a positive factor in her life.

This was further evidenced when Emily's 25-year-old teacher wrote Judy a note. She shared that she was adopted and how much she appreciated hearing Emily speak about her open adoption. Her description of Emily's delivery was that "Emily explained her adoption eloquently." The teacher herself had always had questions about her birthfamily and no avenue for knowledge. She remarked that Emily had a clearer sense of self than she had. She further said she was glad Emily felt her birthmother's love firsthand. This exchange was a powerful one regarding the impact this 6½ year old had on her teacher. The missing pieces the teacher felt were not a part of Emily's experience.

Knowledge of Birthparents Impacts Self-Image

As is to be expected, when children know their birthfamily they begin to identify attributes within themselves that they recognize in their birthfamily. This is quite common as we look around our family units to hear comments like "He is musical like Uncle Pete." "Big toes run in our family." "I have straight hair like my mother." It is normal to identify with our families in this fashion. Definition of self is impacted by access to knowledge. Obviously children involved with open adoption are no exception to this common practice. They, in fact, identify with both birth and adoptive family members.

Emily has attributed her high level of intelligence to both her parents and birthmother. When she learned Katherine had scored 99th percentile in an aptitude exam, the identification was very rapid.

Emily explains her extra weight by attributing this as a similarity to Katherine. Judy points out to her that her birth-grandmother and great-grandmother are both slim, petite women. Reality basing will assist Emily as she sorts through her eating habits and her body build. Having the information available through personal observation offers opportunities for assessing which behavior she chooses to model.

Emily and her family do not have contact with her birth-father. That is his choice. As such, he is a totally abstract person to Emily. Judy notes, "Emily likes her eyes and she likes Katherine's. Therefore, she says her eyes are like Katherine's. Whereupon, I told her that, while the shape is Katherine's, the deep brown shade is her birthfather's. Emily would not acknowledge that similarity. He is not a reality to her at this point, and she, therefore, is not prepared to attribute her features to him." This is an interesting contrast in identification with her known birthmother vs. her denial of the unknown birthfather's attributes.

Extended Family

Concern is often expressed regarding children dealing with so many extra relationships. It has been our experience that the children interact with extended family comfortably. The degree of intimacy is more determined by affinity than anything else.

Emily

Emily has had contact with Katherine's grandmother, Madge, since she was 2 years old. Katherine and Madge have a very close relationship. Emily calls her Grandma Madge. This is a grandma she doesn't see frequently, but someone who always remembers her, especially at birthday time and Christmas. Emily loves to open her gifts when they arrive. Judy uses this opportunity to discuss the giver. Judy, who is keenly aware of developmental stages in children, notes, "Because of Emily's stage of development, she is still very concrete in her thinking. Therefore, physical things (e.g., gifts) represent love. These gifts are evidence of love in ways she can understand."

When asked how Emily interacts with Grandma Madge, Judy responds, "Madge is very sensitive to Emily's cues, and Emily has not wanted physical contact like hugs and kisses. Madge respects this." In gentle ways she is nurturing the relationship while respecting boundaries. There has been evidence of Emily's positive feelings through comments made by her when they read a book sent by Madge or when she chooses to wear a special T-shirt decorated for her. Acknowledged as a loved grandchild, Emily will internalize the positive messages and interact in ways comfortable to her. In the meantime, regularity of contact yields familiarity.

Andy

Lorraine and Bill have maintained contact with Andy's birthmother over the years. Meetings, including the extended family, took place while she lived in the same city. When she married and moved, they stayed in touch through correspondence. When Andy was 9, he asked to see his birthmother. He couldn't remember the earlier meetings, as he had been fairly young. After a phone call, a meeting was arranged which included his birthmother, her children, her mother, and her sister. They had a wonderful, lighthearted visit. Andy absorbed their reality and was satisfied. Lorraine feels that as each year passes, Andy understands more about his adoption. Lorraine and Bill feel fortunate to be able to be forthright and honest with him. They also feel that the openness takes a burden off of them as parents, as they are able to face that part of their life directly and honestly. They are pleased to observe that Andy freely tells his friends and others about his birthfamily. Including the extended family is a natural step for all of them.

Most importantly, each family member provides Andy with a different dimension of his heritage, giving him a further sense of self and genetic history.

As evidenced by Emily and Andy, when extended family is available to participate in the adoption experience, they contribute to the sense of connectedness of the child. Each family member is a branch of the very important family tree to which the child belongs.

Birthparents—Inconsistent Contact

As mentioned previously, one of the most significant problems reported with open adoption is inconsistent contact on the part of the birthparents. The children of open adoption become accustomed to visits or correspondence and are deeply hurt, sad, or angry when contact diminishes or is inconsistent.

Eric Wunsche is 6 years old. His sister, Kirsten, age 8, has a great deal of contact with her birthparents. Meetings are arranged as frequently as possible (given that they do not live in the same state) and contact is fairly regular. Eric has felt hurt and disappointment because recently his birthmother, Lee, has not been able to cope with ongoing contact. She loves him and continues to care but chooses to limit interaction due to factors in her life. Eric visited with Lee when he was pre-school age, and he cannot understand why she no longer visits.

Eric's mom, Betty, recalls their last visit to Texas, when Kirsten visited with her birthmother, and Eric kept hoping to see Lee. Betty remembers asking Eric to pick up the phone before they headed home. With a grin on his face, he said, "I know who it is, it's Lee." Unfortunately, it wasn't, and he was deeply disappointed. The visit had come and gone, and Lee had not accepted their invitation for contact. A few months later his birthmother's name was mentioned, and Eric told his mom he didn't like Lee. This comment was followed by a discussion about liking and being disappointed. "He decided he was mad at her," Betty writes. "I recognize Lee's right to close off communication. I hurt for Eric, who sees the openness his sister has and is too young to understand Lee's behavior. I'm afraid for Eric. I'm afraid he will experience Lee's reaction as rejection and internalize the hurt without talking about it or working it through." Betty works hard at helping Eric verbalize his feelings, while not being judgmental of Lee. Still, it is painful to witness her child's feelings. She also feels there is pent up anger that is difficult to diffuse without contact. This is evident to her in Eric's behavior.

The Wunsches decided to use a third party to assist with Eric's emotional needs, in addition to including him in Kirsten's experience. On their next visit to Texas they arranged a meeting with the adoption professional who had worked with Lee over several years. She told Eric how much Lee loves him and how pleased she is to hear about him. Eric doesn't understand why Lee doesn't see him. It is hard for a six-year-old to make sense of this inability on her part. Still, a person who has had direct contact with Lee provided a concrete message of ongoing love and being remembered. Hopefully, this will hold Eric for an interval of time. In a trusting and loving fashion, he sent Lee a big hug and kiss by personally delivering this to the intermediary. He beamed at the knowledge that it would reach Lee.

It is difficult for all who care to witness the unmet needs of these children. Still, having the opportunity to have it out in the open makes it possible for them to be validated and supported. This, in itself, is a valuable therapeutic intervention. The parents' role here is to validate the child and help him process his feelings. It is impossible to eliminate the hurt. However, one can be understanding, comforting, and nonjudgmental. In simple terms, the child can be helped to begin to absorb the complexities of birthparenthood. Parents who show love and compassion for the birthparents' dilemma will serve the child well in this difficult experience.

Birthparents, take note—your role cannot be filled by another. As life is created, it needs emotional nurturing, particularly by significant persons. This does not cease with adoption. The child's long-term well-being depends on his clear knowledge that he is loved and remembered by his first parents. Therefore, it is important for adoption professionals who are facilitating open adoptions to educate birthparents about the long-term needs of the child and the importance of consistent contact over the years. In fact, it should be pointed out to birthparents that if there is to be contact over the years, it is their *responsibility* to maintain that contact on a consistent basis for the benefit and mental health of the child.

Unexpected Sentiments

Janie and her husband had included their children's birthparents in their life since the adoption took place. Contact included all forms of communication—letters, phone calls, and visits. These occurred at comfortable intervals, typically around birthday time and holidays. Intermittent visits occurred as opportune for all concerned. All reported being comfortable with the flow of contact over the years. When her son was 6 years old, he said he loved his mom and birthmom just the same. Janie experienced a hurt she had not anticipated. It shocked her that her son had those feelings.

Discussing her own feelings with her social worker, she was able to reframe the experience. Instead of being in competition with the birthmother, she was able to see what a good job she had done of freeing her son up to tell her he loved both his mothers. He obviously had received messages that expressing this out loud was permissible in his home. What a credit to the communication lines within this family.

Another adoptive mother, Deanna, candidly states:

> I did have to adjust to having my children express love for their birthparents, but I kept reminding myself that I have enough love for more than one, why shouldn't they. As has proven with all aspects of openness for us, the more freely we express ourselves with honesty, the easier it gets, whether it is expressions of love, discussing adoption, and any and all feelings and processes of growing up.

Adoptive parents have the task, as all parents do, of responding to their children's needs even when those needs seem to threaten the unique relationship they have with their child. After all, the task of parenthood is to prepare to let go. In open adoption we observe a diminished possessiveness on the part of adoptive parents. As they acknowledge the reality of the birthparents, they seem to have a more relaxed parenting style than their often fearful and possessive closed adoption counterparts.

Witnessing Affinity and Personality Similarities

Adoptive parents involved with open adoption often report that interaction with birthparents provides them with important information about their children. Ben and Kay, whose son, John, is 6 years old, have had ongoing visits three or four times a year with John's birthmother since he was an infant. John's parents observe a multitude of personality traits and behavioral patterns that are shared by John and his birthmother.

Kay reports that witnessing these allows her to better interact with John as it gives her a better understanding of what makes him "tick." The demonstrated genetic attributes in all of this enhances the parent-child relationship and increases the "goodness of fit" often alluded to in adoption. They report feeling wonder as they behold the similarities between child and birthparent. Witnessing these has benefited them in dealing with their reality as a family by adoption.

Another mother shared her emotional journey as she witnessed the obvious affinity and great resemblance between her 6-year-old and her birthmother. This family had opted for ongoing visitation from the very beginning, feeling it was the only healthy path for all. She reported feeling badly when she witnessed this affinity and resemblance in spite of the conviction for continued contact.

Exploration of this area is vitally important. In this person's case it may have to do with entitlement issues or even the ongoing process of infertility grief. Her emotional response will undoubtedly guide her messages, verbal and nonverbal, to her children. Another mother shared that when her 9-year-old insists that her birthmother is her "real" mother that she says "No, *I'm* your real mother." She further stated that she will periodically say to her daughter, "Aren't you glad you are adopted?"

This mother has issues to work out even as a participant in the open-adoption journey. Fortunately, she seeks guidance from adoption professionals so that she can process her feelings. One hopes that the outcome will then be a change in the script she uses with her daughter. For example, when her child says "my birthmother is my 'real' mother", she can affirm them both by saying "we are both 'real'—I am the mother raising you and she is your birthmother who loves you too."

She hopefully will also change her script from "aren't you glad you are adopted" (which seems to be asking for affirmation from the child for being a parent) to "I'm so glad we adopted you." The message takes on a totally different significance, conveying a totally different level of comfort. In this vein, Laurie Morkert shares Cara's experience with the "realness" of her two mothers:

> Cara (age 8) knows that Ann and Greg gave birth to her. At times the term "real parents" is confusing for her—she sees both Ann and me as her "real" mothers—and we both are, but in different ways. Sometimes when Cara has been *extremely* upset with me, she will state that she wants to go live with Ann. The first time she said this it hurt, but I was able to share with her that I thought Ann would also handle a similar situation the same way, and if Cara wanted to, we could write to Ann and ask her. This totally diffused the intensity of the situation for both of us.

Another family of school-age girls involved in this issue of "realness" reported that their two daughters, Katherine (age 8) and Jennifer (age 6), took turns when angry, stating that their mom was not their real mom. Each time, the situation was handled calmly, exhibiting no push of the famous "button." Each time the mother affirmed herself as real, while indicating what her expectations were for their behavior. Affirmations were stated later of "We are a permanent unit."

Intrinsic in the "You're not my real mother" message are a variety of issues:

> There is the need for reassurance that, indeed, mother is the real parent, which embodies permanence.

The message of permanence has to do with the adoptee's fear of losing the parents they have after having gone through the original loss of birthparents.

There is also an underlying need to have acknowledged the reality of two sets of parents—each with its own role.

It is of great importance that parents be aware of all these dimensions in dealing with the "real-parent" issue. When children see parents coping without hurt, they are better able to move on and internalize everyone's realness.

Katherine and Jennifer, after a period of challenging the realness of their mother, finally reached a point of correcting each other. The message was, "She *is* your mother, and she *can* tell you what to do." This was such a confirmation for the previous calm handling of the situation. After a period of time, the "real" vs. "not real" episodes ended.

When There Are Siblings: Contact and Knowledge

The issue of birth siblings and how to tell adopted children about them is often an area of concern, both for adoptive parents and birthparents. This usually stems from the fear that the adopted child will feel greater rejection when he learns that older or younger siblings are with the birthparent.

Adult adopted individuals often report wondering, as children, whether they had siblings. Sometimes this involved, indeed, once again, examining the significance of adoption as it relates to love versus rejection. More often than not, however, the focus shifted to an interest in knowing whether siblings existed and to a desire to know these individuals.

Bearing this in mind, we encourage adoptive parents to be truthful with their children when older siblings exist or subsequent ones are born. Initially, it is desirable to describe these siblings as the "birthmother's children" as opposed to labelling them as "*your* sister/brother." This latter labelling has the potential for confusion in a very young child. Our experience has demonstrated that as children learn about relationships during the preschool years, they make the connection integrating that birthmother Mary's child is also a sister/brother. This level of understanding is usually followed by a comfortable peace with the knowledge. As a matter of fact, a great deal of enthusiasm is usually demonstrated when pictures arrive or personal contact occurs between siblings.

Suzanne, age 7, wrote the following letter:

Dear Linda

I love you very very very very mutch
I also miss you
how is my new birth sister
how are you and your husband
Well I got to go.
By.

Love
Suzanne

If it is discerned that the adopted child is expressing concern about the sibling living with the birthparent, adoptive parents and birthparents should take this opportunity to further communicate about adoption facts and feelings. Often expressed is the fact that the birthparent did the best she could at that time in her life when the adoption occurred.

Brian

Brian, age 9, learned his birthmother was now married and had two boys. He was excited to learn about these boys, saying he had always wanted a younger brother. His birthmother indicated that her sons did not know about Brian but that someday she would tell them.

The telling happened sooner than expected, as she writes to his parents:

Thank you very much for letting Brian write. It meant a lot to me to see his handwriting and a picture of him.

It's alright for him to write to Stephen because I told him about Brian. He knows and understands that Brian has different parents. Stephen wanted to make a birthday card for Brian to wish him a Happy Birthday.

It makes me happy that he has good Christian parents.

Thank you again,
Lynn

Stephen, his birthmother's son, even wrote him a card, which pleased Brian:

Happy Birthday!
I hope you have fun! And be happy and have lots of fun!
Love,
Stephen (age 8)

Later, Brian said he would like to meet his brothers and be friends. He indicated he wanted to write Stephen back, but had not gotten around to it. The message he conveyed was one of satisfaction. He knew they were there for him and this degree of contact was sufficient for now.

Katherine

When Katherine learned that her birthmother had children she was rearing, she was interested in seeing pictures of these children. When she was 5 years old, news arrived that Cindy was expecting, whereupon Katherine said, "She's pregnant again! She's going to have 3 kids. She's going to go crazy!" It was stated as an observation and no distress was evidenced.

When she was 6, she said regretfully, "I wish Cindy's husband was my birthfather." It was time to process grief-related emotions. She reasoned, without having to elaborate out loud, that Cindy and her husband were raising their children together. If she had been born to them, she would probably have remained with them. During these discussions, it is again important for the parent to provide support as the emotions are experienced and adoption realities are being digested. Working towards acceptance of one's reality becomes the underlying goal.

Katherine's stage of fantasizing about possible outcomes lasted for a while. Over the span of two years this issue arose periodically. A major turning point was reached when expressions of regret ceased and a marked acceptance—verbalized, even—was reached. Like other adoption cycles, it may recur. In the meantime, a peace has settled over her being. This turn of events was greatly aided by the love expressed by both sets of parents. The contact with Cindy helped her move through the conflict period. Realities helped deal with the fantasies of what might have been. It would be too simplistic to say this will never recur. Contact will again be used as a tool for processing, when needed.

Telling Birth Siblings About Adoption

Shirley chose to tell her daughter Karen, age 11, about Jason—the child adopted by Jim and Evelyn. Karen responded enthusiastically to the information that she had a brother. Her own level of development was such that she didn't understand all of the complexities of adoption. She very much wants to meet Jason and include him in their family. It is still difficult for her to understand why this doesn't happen. Shirley acknowledges that this aspect is difficult for her to witness. However, she doesn't regret telling Karen and strives to help her understand. Karen has written Jason, defusing some of her frustration regarding contact. She wrote the following:

Dear Jason,

Hi! How have you been? As for me, fine. I have never seen you before. I have never forgotten your birthday because it is so special to me. My birthday is Feb. 15. I am 11 years old. Mom says that you are very smart. I am. I am, too. I am a patrol. I just became the first girl captain. Mom also says you are a very good reader. Just like me. My teacher says I am, so I agree. I wonder when I am going to see you. I'm looking forward to this day. Even though I haven't seen you, I can say that I love you. I relly don't have to see you to say that because me and my heart already knows it. Mom also told me that you were excited about having a sister. I'm glad you're knowing more about Mom and me. Well, I really have to go now. Bye. Bye.

Love,
Your sister, Karen

P.S. I hope you will write back. I'd like that.

Tiffany, 9 years old, wrote the following to her birth brother, age, 17, who is adopted:

Oh! Nathan can I have a picture of you? All the pictures of you I have is when your 13 & 16 okay.

Love you
Tiffany.

We have observed that girl siblings tend to be more effusive in their communication. Obviously when contact is purely through correspondence fantasies abound, and correspondence tends to reflect a flavor of letters written to a teen idol (or to a greatly admired person).

When Adoptive Parents Give Birth

What is the impact on an adopted child when a sibling is born to his adoptive parents? Often reported are feelings of jealousy, fear of losing one's place in the family, and insecurity. These feelings are typical in any family whenever a new child is added. However, we have all heard comments made regarding changes in feelings for the adopted child once the "real" child is born. This is a painful exchange for both adoptive parents and adopted children. The impact of open adoption has been felt here also as children develop feelings of trust and permanence through contact with birthparents.

Lorraine and Bill have two sons by adoption. Their family further expanded when their daughter, Kelly, was born 5 years ago. Lorraine observes that having open adoption has positively impacted on the processing the boys have done regarding how each child entered the family.

Kelly, inquisitive about her birth, likes to watch the video tape featuring her arrival into the world. Sensitive to Chris and Andy, Lorraine uses the opportunity to tell them about their birth. Her observation is that the boys' differences are diminished because of the available information. She has witnessed no evidence of distress or insecurity. Rather, she believes that they are at peace with how their family was formed.

Lorraine remarked that outsiders periodically will scrutinize Kelly's features and identify them with her mom or dad. She feels grateful to have pictures of the boys' birthfamilies, so they, too, may identify their characteristics. Again, the differences among the children diminish.

Divorce and Open Adoption

Divorce is a reality in our society. It is known that loss and grief are two major ingredients when a divorce occurs. Children who have been adopted have already experienced loss and grief. Divorce revisits these issues and forces the child, whether verbally and/or emotionally, to deal with these again, now in a new context.

Families involved in openness have the advantage that the child has had verification of love and caring from their birthparents over the years at a very real level. This allows them to work through their grief and loss issues over time, while integrating adoption realities. Instead of intense feelings of abandonment and rejection, they are able to internalize feelings of love, permanence, and trust. This will, in turn, impact on how they handle emotions brought on by divorce. It is understood in the professional arena that new losses bring about a revisiting of previous losses.

When these losses are at a greater degree of resolution, the new loss is better dealt with. This does not mean that divorce is not a painful experience. Of course, it is. However, when contrasting children of closed adoption with children of open adoption, the latter demonstrate a heightened capacity to confront the pain of divorce.

Open Adoption—Losing Contact

Our society is a mobile one. As such, geographical distances create barriers to communication. The majority of the United States still embraces traditional adoption as the norm. New friends and neighbors are frequently appalled by accountings of relationships embodying openness. The result is that some adoptive parents not only lose the ongoing feedback from the birthparents regarding the effects of contact, but they lose the broad experience base of their support group (the adoption intermediary and other participants). Sometimes this leads to a backing off, so as not to offend, hurt, or disturb birthparents. Contact may go from ongoing person-to-person interaction to infrequent communication.

This situation was experienced by Nancy and Terry Snider. Their two children, Drew, age 9, and Sarah, age 7, have open adoptions which have included ongoing visitation with Sarah's birthmother, Gloria. When the Sniders left Texas and moved to Pennsylvania, correspondence became the norm. As time passed, they no longer heard from Gloria in response to their yearly Christmas cards. In reflecting over this state of affairs, they wondered if Gloria had decided to phase out. Not wanting to offend her or overstep, they wondered but never addressed the issue with her. Sarah is presently very inquisitive about her birthmother and her adoption in general.

In consulting with their social worker in Texas, they agreed it would be wise to have the social worker approach Gloria directly. Openness provides avenues that can minimize guessing. They discovered that Gloria was not able (for personal reasons) to participate at this time. Instead, contact was facilitated with her sister and mother. Sarah was responded to by providing links to her birthfamily. The Sniders were also able to get an update that was factual, and they learned that Gloria is always pleased to hear from them. They look toward to the day when contact will be renewed with her. In the meantime, they plan to continue corresponding through her mother. They no longer have to wonder about what is going on. Sarah demonstrates a comfort level with this new knowledge.

The School-Age Years in Review

We have witnessed how school-age children are dealing with various dimensions of the open-adoption experience. The greater the degree of openness, the less fantasizing that takes place and the more the issues are worked on. Children demonstrate a strong desire for contact with their birthparents. The resulting heightened comfort level with adoption nurtures feelings of self-esteem and entitlement within both families. The honest acknowledgment of their reality assists them in the areas of adoption understanding, bonding, grief, communication, and emotional well-being. All members of the adoption triangle benefit from this process, striving together to achieve common goals of self-actualization.

□ 7 □

THE TEENAGE YEARS

The adolescent years are typically difficult ones for any youngster and his family. It is a time of searching for self, assertiveness, and individuation. Add the adoption experience and the complexity of these years multiplies.

Many parents have questioned the wisdom of facilitating contact with the birthfamily during the teenage years—the fear being that this is a difficult enough period without adding the complication and/or confusion related to the birthparent connection. Overlooked in this fear is the fact that the child of closed adoption has grappled blindly with adoption issues all through the childhood and preteenage years. How can one clearly define self when it is done without an awareness of past generations? How can one look forward to his future when he has no sense of the past?

We have worked with many teens who began contact with their birthparents during the preteen years, as well as those whose contact began during the teen years themselves. We will examine what led their parents to permit this contact and what the impact has been.

To date, we do not have experience with teenagers who have experienced open adoption from infancy. But we can already predict, based on the experiences of preschool and school-age children with open adoptions, that the children of open adoption will fare better in adolescence than those with traditional adoption. Even the teenagers we will discuss in this chapter who initiated openness in adolescence have fared better than those with closed adoptions. Traditional adoption "wisdom " (and laws) have frequently prevented agencies and helping professionals from aiding children and teenagers open up closed adoptions until they reach the magic age of adulthood. We question and challenge that conventional "wisdom" and practice, as we are convinced that children need openness—their very mental health depends on it. We encourage adoption agencies to open up closed adoptions when requested to do so by adoptive parents, birthparents, and children, as the stories in this chapter will demonstrate.

Grief and Loss—The Teen Years

We have stated that grief and loss issues are in evidence at an early age. These issues often take on a renewed intensity in the teen years. During this developmental stage, youngsters are separating from their parents. This very normal phenomena often causes distress related to the prospect of losing the relationship with their parents. Having already experienced a major loss—that of their birthparents and birthfamily—they must once again face a separation that leads to that less protected status of adulthood. Growing up can, therefore, be frightening.

Sometimes the original loss has such a strong impact that teenagers, consciously or unconsciously, refuse to separate from their parents. They stay in a prolonged dependency state inappropriate for young adults. An example would be a self-supporting adult who doesn't set up his own household but, instead, remains a resident at his parents' home. Another example would be someone who never seems to get it together financially and ends up being subsidized by his parents. It behooves parents to be alert to these patterns of dependency which leave the parents in the eternal caretaker role.

Understanding the contribution of adoption to these dynamics can help a family effectively deal with this so that the young adult becomes securely independent in an appropriate fashion. The growing independence must be encouraged during the teen years. At the same time, explicit assurance of continued love and connection becomes vital when this process is taking place.

Sometimes we see teens coping with loss through the use of defenses, such as rejection and denial. This becomes manifested when someone says, "I don't give a hoot about my birthmother. She gave me up, and I have no need for her." Statements of this sort often are a cover-up of the hurts brought about by the separation through adoption. We have found, in working with adopted individuals, that the armour of self-protection diminishes when verification of continued caring comes from the birthparents. The need for protection of feelings seems to be greater in males than females. In our culture, girls and women are groomed to be in touch with their feelings. Males are conditioned to be more careful regarding the display of feelings. These patterns spill over into the adoption experience, where they already feel vulnerable. We have found that all the manifestations of loss are the same for both genders when there is trust that allows for the access and expression of these feelings.

Acting out behavior during the teenage years is also related to loss. Running away from home is a way that the young person searches for his birthparents. It is often a symbolic quest which combines within it the teen's power to leave his parents just as he was left by his original parents. The approach–avoidance often seen in teens who repeatedly run away and return demonstrates the internal confusion they feel. They search for the lost parent, and they run away from and return to the known parents. Closed adoption reinforces the maintenance of this internal havoc. Through openness, adolescents have a sense of permanence regarding both sets of parents, which diminishes the need for running-away patterns.

Other negative behaviors associated with loss include ones that seem to invite rejection from the adoptive parents. Mild to severe deviant behavior challenges the parent–child relationship. During the teen years, peer influence is at its greatest. This, combined with adoption dynamics, can make for a tremendous testing ground regarding the permanence of the parent–child relationship. The adolescent may test the parent to see how far he must go before he is rejected. Intertwined in all of this is the residual childhood notion that the original reason for his adoption was his fault—he was bad, noisy, ugly, etc. This carries over to "If I'm bad enough they surely will send me back, reject me," and so on.

It is especially important that parents have strong parenting skills, including the ability to clearly set limits. They must also be strong communicators so as to express what are acceptable behaviors and what the consequences are for unacceptable behavior. This will help the child know that his relationship with his parents is not tenuous and that behavior will be addressed appropriately for the well-being of the family.

Sadness as an expression of loss is also manifested by many. Janna said that for as long as she could remember birthdays were hard for her. For years she stayed up until her birthtime on her birthday. This meant staying up until the wee hours of the night. This was a very private ritual which included a great deal of sadness and longing for those faceless birthparents. She wondered if her birthmother ever thought of her or remembered her. A great deal of energy was expended on these issues. Janna was contacted by her birthparents when she was 19 years old. Years of wondering and longing came to a halt. She was now able to concretely absorb her birthparents' reality and use her energies elsewhere. The loss was gradually replaced by feelings of wholeness and well-being. Where her life had been lacking direction, she now was able to identify more realistic goals. It is important not to over-simplify the nature of contact. Loss continues to play a part. This time it is related to the lost opportunity to share the preceding years. However, intertwined in this is the hope for a present and future relationship. This makes the lost years more bearable. Sometimes the individuals involved are surprised by the intensity of these feelings. In this regard, the teen years bring an awareness (of the lost years) that does not appear to be present in younger children.

"Who am I?" is a central question during the teen years. Unavailability of answers deepens the sense of loss. Our sense of self is defined not only by our present but also by our past. Through closed adoption our past becomes inaccessible. We have found in working with teens that the tasks of adolescence are better accomplished when there is access to their birthfamilies. Loss issues are addressed and emotionally processed. This is the case even when contact wasn't possible from the beginning. We have found that facilitating contact between a teen and his birthparent assists in the processing of adoption grief. This allows the adolescent to move on in his personal development.

Teenagers and Openness—
From Latency to Adolescence

When Nathan was 11, Kathy (his birthmother) approached the agency that had handled his adoption. She felt the need to make herself available to his family and to know that he was alright. Betty (his mom) understood her need and promptly entered into correspondence with Kathy.

Nathan's parents shared this turn of events with him. Nathan was very excited and wanted to invite Kathy and her family to dinner. Responding to these cues, his parents presented him with pictures of Kathy on his twelfth birthday. They were startled by his response. His mood quickly became one of anger. His parents couldn't understand the change. Now 17, Nathan looks back on this episode and states that the pictures shocked him, and he didn't like getting them on his birthday. In retrospect, Betty felt that perhaps the pictures held too much reality. Kathy was a real flesh-and-bones person. Nathan had to confront some of his feelings more concretely. He wasn't able or willing to share why this bothered him. Nathan did say, however, that these feelings of anger subsided, and he felt better over time, especially after he himself began to get letters from Kathy. These usually arrive right around his birthday. Occasionally, a letter will arrive at other times.

When asked how he feels about contact, Nathan said it has been "pretty cool." In some ways he feels he wasn't ready for the contact when he was 12, but now he is glad his mother kept up the correspondence with Kathy. Betty, sensitive to Nathan, writes:

> After Nathan's last birthday card (17 years) I asked if the letters or cards were disturbing to him, and he said, "sometimes." I asked if he wanted it stopped, and he said no. I asked him if it was okay with him if I kept in contact with Kathy, and he said yes.

Nathan doesn't feel the need to increase the contact with Kathy at this time. He thinks some years down the road he might choose to meet her. When asked how he perceives Kathy, he says he considers her a friend. He doesn't feel any loyalty struggle. To him, his mom is mom. He predicts that after he meets Kathy, she will continue to be identified as a friend. For the time being, he is comfortable receiving her letters, but that is the extent of it. He has written back once.

It is important to respect the pacing that a teenager is comfortable with. To push any more contact would be counterproductive. When Nathan is ready for more, he will have the opportunity to express himself. In the meantime, he and Kathy are building some trust between them that is respectful of his needs.

Sometimes teenagers have emotions they are not ready to deal with. The teen years are intense enough on their own. Readiness to confront adoption issues is determined by personal timing. The advantage of contact with birthparents is that when the individual is ready to deal with his emotions, he can do so with those significant in his adoption experience.

Betty comments on the benefits of openness for parents during the teen years:

> The benefit of being open is that "It" is out in the open and if someone wants to say something or feel something it's okay. There is pain and joy and anger.
>
> I have good feelings when sharing with Kathy. Seems the least I can do—she gave me a son. And who could have more in common than two mothers of the same child? We both know how special he is . . . By being open I feel Nathan had a good chance to know and understand what adoption is.
>
> I don't feel threatened by the birthparents. At one time the thoughts did go through my mind, Oh my, what if he'd want to go live with Kathy? The fear just went away. I'm pleased to see that Nathan cares about Kathy and her daughter.

When Is a Teen Ready?

Defining readiness for contact on the part of a teen is usually a function of parental comfort with all that adoption entails. Many parents report that their children have barraged them with questions since early childhood. Usually answers were limited to the information obtained at the time of the adoption. Parents at ease with adoption communication conveyed to their children over the years that they would assist them in their quest for knowledge. The timing for this was often conveyed as some indefinite future point. The willingness to help was there, but there were no available paths for access. As adoption agencies began to provide openness options at the time of placement, parents of teens came forward to inquire if they, too, could use these services.

The typical adoptive parent approaching an agency for information is one who sees the need for his child to obtain the information now, rather than in the future. There is a sense of security regarding the bond between the parent and child. Additionally, there is a willingness to risk during a developmental stage that embodies many complexities.

When such a request for contact is initiated, it is important for an adoption counselor to meet with the family to discuss the typical issues which may arise. The preparation is much like that done for adults searching for birthparents. Among the topics covered, in an age appropriate way, are:

expectations regarding contact

fantasies regarding birthparents

loyalty issues pertaining to adoptive parents and
    birthparents

what one calls birthparents

dealing with emotions regarding the "lost" years

maximizing communication among participants

respect of boundaries

This preparation is particularly important for the teenager who developmentally is focused on the present. The pleasure of the moment must be combined with a responsible look forward to the future. It is too painful for birthparents to be contacted, quizzed for information, and then dropped, as teens pursue other teenage endeavors. Rather than plunge into an immediate physical contact upon location of birthparents, we typically facilitate correspondence for as long as seems appropriate to lay the groundwork for long-term benefit.

Guidance is sought from the participants regarding the pacing of this process. Parents provide feedback from the adult perspective regarding their child's handling of the correspondence. Their involvement and support also becomes a crucial ingredient in freeing the adolescent to participate without the loyalty struggles and guilt so often found in searching adult adoptees. Through their involvement and input, the adoptive parents are also given their rightful role as the guiding force for their child (entitlement revisited). We have found that these adolescents are very comfortable with the correspondence stage, as it serves as a buffer while they are getting acquainted. They often will say, in retrospect, that it really helped to do this and not jump into an immediate meeting, as they originally had wanted.

In fact, correspondence tends to allow for emotional dosages that seem to be better managed. Too intense interaction—like a whirlwind love affair— seems to frighten and overwhelm this age group. Actually, we frequently see this phenomenon when adopted adults make contact with birthparents for the first time. When the intensity becomes hard to manage, the outcome is distancing—both physical and emotional.

Whenever correspondence ceases to be satisfying and the personal meeting becomes the next step, preparation and support are again important ingredients. Both the adoptive family and the birthparents are individually assisted to examine again the typical issues that arise through physical contact. As in the case of the preschool and school-age child, when a meeting takes place the support of the adoptive parents is important. If there is a facilitator, he is more likely to help break the ice through introductions and a brief exchange, and then allow the group to meet privately. The teen is less vulnerable than the younger child and by now has done a lot of work building a relationship with the birthparent.

These first meetings last approximately one to one and a half hours, as all parties enthusiastically share with one another, as well as absorb physical realities. These meetings tend to be fairly lighthearted, though emotions, of course, are exhibited. After the meeting, the counselor facilitates processing again with all parties. This is an important sharing time between adoptive parents and the adolescent—a time to hear one another verbalize how the meeting felt. This also becomes a time of confirmation of their family unit, while integrating the birthmother at a higher degree of reality.

A Door Is Opened to the Future

Fourteen years after the adoption of her child, Robin approached her agency. All those years that had passed had been laden with fear that her daughter was not well. She came forward to obtain knowledge of her daughter's well-being.

At her request, the adoptive parents were contacted through the social worker. Her daughter's obviously adoring mother shared a multitude of details about her child. Every characteristic was illustrated by an anecdote. Copious notes were taken of this telephone exchange so obviously loaded with empathy for the birthmother. When told the information, Robin said to the social worker, "You have just made my day. You have just made my year. You have just made my last 14 years. I feel like I have gone to the moon!"

The years passed with no further contact until Janet, the adoptive mom, notified the agency that they had recently shared with their daughter the birthmother's inquiry. Jill, now 16, had expressed delight and a desire to know more. Now the wheels turned to facilitate the contact requested by the adoptive parents. The seeds had been planted some years before with the knowledge that contact was possible.

Janet is the epitome of the mother who profoundly loves her child, as evidenced in this letter to Jill's birthmother:

> I am Jill's mother. I am not worried about our relationship or that of the rest of the family. She is also

> very secure with our relationship. I hope and pray that you will be her friend . . . I know this cannot be easy for you, my heart goes out to you. I have thought of you often as I have watched Jill grow up . . . She is loved by everyone. I know you'll be delighted.

Jill and her birthmother corresponded a few times. Due to circumstances in her life, Robin does not feel ready to maintain regular contact or to meet them. This has been a source of disappointment and hurt to Jill and her family.

Robin writes:

> . . . Believe me when I say that hearing that you have had a wonderful and loving family makes me happier than anyone will ever know. The letter I received from your mother was such a joy, it helped fill in the blanks. . . .

To the social worker she wrote. " . . . I want her to understand it isn't her, it's me. . . . But I do care very much. . . . "

However, openness in adoption does embody a respect for mutual readiness, and Jill looks forward to the day when mutuality exists. In the meantime, Jill has taken some steps to establish a link with her birthgrandparents. It all happened rather unexpectedly. Jill's adoptive grandma invited her and her two cousins to visit San Antonio as a graduation gift for all three girls. Included in their itinerary was some time with the social worker who had been the intermediary. Upon learning of her visit through the social worker, her birthgrandparents expressed an interest in meeting. Jill wanted that, too. Consultations followed with her mother, her adoptive grandmother, and even her cousins, as this had not been part of the original plan, and sensitivity to all was important.

The social worker spent time preparing the birthgrandparents for the visit, and even met with a birthaunt. It was important to examine the many complexities of contact, especially one so unexpected. Everyone demonstrated an enthusiastic readiness. The meeting took place at the motel where Jill and her family were staying. Her protective grandma felt it was important to be present, as she was responsible for her grand-daughter's well-being.

Thus evolved a meeting that included grandparents from both family trees that Jill belongs to. It was a very emotional visit with many tears and many laughs. The birthgrandparents, Maureen and Joe, put everyone at ease with their relaxed Texas manner. They told anecdote after anecdote while Jill absorbed them. The intensity diminished as everyone present partici-pated. The gathering lasted approximately three hours, with everyone feeling satisfied that this was the right thing to do.

Later Jill wrote to the social worker, "I hope they (her birthgrandparents) know how much I appreciate all they told me and that I wouldn't have missed meeting them for any-thing." And to her birthgrandparents, she wrote:

> Let me say how glad I was to meet you. It's a lot eas-ier for me to write to you now that I have met you. It was so interesting to see how similar my eyes are to yours, Maureen. I have always wondered who I looked like; where my dark eyes came from. Thank you so much for sharing all those special stories with me about Robin. I've always wondered what kind of things she liked to do as a child and as an adult.
>
> Thank you again for giving me the picture of Robin. It really means a lot to me, especially because it's the only picture I have of her, but also because she was about my age when the picture was taken.

The months passed and no further contact occurred between Jill and her birthgrandparents. She developed feelings of anger that they had not responded to her letter. In many ways, she felt rejected. Her family gave her loving support dur-ing this time.

Unfortunately, a lack of clear communication created this stressful situation. It was later discovered that the silence on their part was to give her time to settle in to her first year of college. Additionally, Maureen admitted to being a terrible cor-respondent. The phone was her preferred mode of communi-cation. The clarification paved the way for renewed contact, and one hopes this time with clearer communication. As in many other situations, forthright communication becomes a vital ingredient.

When Maureen and Joe were asked how Robin felt about their contact with Jill, the immediate response was, "Great!" Robin has continued her silence, but her silence is not for lack of caring.

From Closed to Open— Adoptive Parent Initiated

One family who journeyed through the process were the Clements. Their daughter, Wendy, had had millions of questions since she was a little girl. When she was fifteen, they approached their agency to seek assistance in contacting Wendy's birthmother.

Wendy is a very stable, well-grounded teenager. Her need to know about herself had intensified. Her parents recognized this and chose to respond to her request. It must be emphasized that her need to know was in no way pathological. It was purely a normal outcome of a closed adoption where answers to questions had never been available—answers that 99% of the population has access to. She wanted to know what her birthmother was like, what she looked like, who she (Wendy) resembled, etc. All of her questions were very normal for an adopted person. She wasn't fixated on adoption. She just wanted to know.

Since so little information had been given to her family at the time of the adoption, a summary was prepared regarding the events leading up to Wendy's adoption. Included in this were papers that had her footprints and other meaningful items. Wendy and her parents were very excited to finally have some of their questions answered.

Shortly thereafter, her birthmother, Barbara, was located and contacted by the social worker. She expressed tremendous appreciation to Wendy's parents for giving her the opportunity to enter Wendy's life at this time. She had always loved Wendy and hoped the day would come when contact would happen. She had never imagined it would be so soon. They had the opportunity to get acquainted through letters for approximately one year. The correspondence included Wendy, her mom, Irene, Barbara, and Barbara's mother. During this time the letter exchange covered some meaningful occasions including Mother's Day and Wendy's birthday.

Wendy summarizes many emotions as she writes Barbara:

> This is the first Mother's Day card I've ever sent to you. I hope it's as special to you as the birthday card you sent me was to me. Thank you for everything. You're very special to me.
> *Love Ya,*
> *Wendy*

Barbara's first letter to Wendy was written the very first night she was contacted:

> . . . I have no way to tell you of all the emotions that I am feeling right now. I think the most overwhelming emotion is joy . . . God was there when I made that [adoption] decision, and He obviously led you into the caring arms of wonderful parents. I'm so grateful for those two people.

As all parties get acquainted through correspondence, we have seen a comfortable affirmation of each other's role in the teen's life and a desire to share. Wendy's mom, Irene, writes:

> I've had the great pleasure, honor, and best time being Wendy's mom. She is truly a joy and has always been very special. She bubbles over with love and happiness. She is very pretty and has a personality even lovelier.
>
> She has, since the age of five, said she wanted to find you and talk to you. She has never wavered in this as some youngsters tend to do. She is a competent, strong, healthy person, both physically and emotionally. Her father and I support her in this need and feel she can manage this even at "Sweet 16."
>
> We are looking forward to learning more about you and your family and finally meeting you. We owe you a great deal, as you gave us our "first love" child. Thank you!
> *Sincerely,*
> *Irene*

Significant in the relationship that was building among all of these individuals was the fact that both mothers respected each other and invested energy to get acquainted themselves as a separate dimension from their mutual child. They shared perceptions and concerns, working to maintain an open communication. When Wendy was short on time for writing, Irene wrote, "Wendy has finally written. I wanted you to know that Bill and I have done nothing to discourage Wendy from writing. Wendy is a busy young woman."

On another occasion, Wendy reacted protectively when Barbara's mother wrote her, welcoming her as a grandchild and inviting her to call her "Granny." Wendy was not prepared for this inclusion and identified the grandmas she had grown up with as the ones to occupy that slot for her. Barbara wrote to Irene, "I just feel it's important that Wendy realize I am not just one person. She must try to understand that I, too, have a family of my own, just as she does."

Extended family usually are prepared to welcome the adopted person back into the family. Very frequently, though, there is reluctance on the part of the adopted person to plunge into the extended family. There seems to be a need to maximize the time with the birthparent and the siblings. As time passes, other members of the family get integrated. Allowing this time to pass becomes vital so that readiness for contact is reached in a comfortable fashion. Interestingly, Wendy's loving grandma, Irene's mom, said that she felt a weight had been lifted from Wendy's shoulders since contact began. What a lovely way to show approval!

During the correspondence stage, Bill and Irene decided to meet Barbara first and develop another level of trust. While this intermediate step is not always the norm, such a situation is tailored for the individuals involved. Everyone has input into what the path will be.

Bill, Irene, and Barbara were glad to have the time, adult to adult, to discuss future interaction. While initially nervousness is evident, as the meeting progresses everyone relaxes as common goals and excited anticipation become the focus. Irene shared, "I felt threatened by Barbara before meeting her. Since we have met and talked, I know she will do nothing to hurt

Wendy or Wendy's relationship with us. Barbara is cognizant of Wendy's needs and feelings as well as ours."

This meeting was a precursor of the one that took place several months later including Wendy. A year of correspondence had prepared them for this event. Wendy expressed a readiness to meet, and her parents supported her. The meeting was a joyful gathering of people who felt connected and cared about each other. Irene relates:

> I used to worry about losing Wendy, but now I know that Wendy's life is only enhanced by this experience . . . I know I have not been replaced. Wendy and Barbara act like sisters when they are together. They seem to be having fun with their relationship.

Two years have now passed since the Clements and Barbara made contact. All parties are very positive about the nature of the relationship that continues to unfold. Wendy and Barbara see each other as good friends. All of the adults report that Wendy is handling the complex interaction very well, integrating Barbara and her children into her life with ease. She visits in Barbara's home about every three months and talks on the phone two or three times a month. She is not yet ready to immerse herself in Barbara's extended family. Everyone respects her need for pacing herself. Barbara, who lives in another town, also visits Wendy and her family with her children.

Irene states that "Openness has made Wendy a 'valid' person. She has roots; she knows why she looks the way she does. This has been important to her in the 'growing up' concept. Wendy also feels better about herself."

Wendy, talented in poetry, expresses her feelings about adoption in a poem written when she was fifteen:

MOTHER'S REAL LOVE

Part I

Every mother, as you can plainly see,
Wants her daughter to be happy as can be.
I have an interesting tale to tell

That expresses this very well

When she was just seventeen
She gave birth to a baby girl.
She loved this baby very much,
More than anything else in the world.

She decided she didn't have the money or life
To bring her up just right.
So she gave her up for adoption
So she could have a family just right.

I am the baby girl, though not a baby anymore,
And I appreciate this special love.
For it is such a powerful feeling
Sent from God above.

I have a very special family now,
But I admit, I have to inquire
About the woman who gave me life,
Before my life will be entire.

This woman had strength and lots of courage
And lots of help from above.
This woman had a special gift.
She had a mother's real love.

Part II

Another woman who gave me a lot
Is the mother I have now.
She didn't give me life,
But she did fulfill it somehow.

This woman is who I call "Mom,"
The only "Mom" I know,
I love her very much,
And I hope that I let it show.

She and my family mean more to me
Than anything else in the world,
And I hope she will always think

Of me as HER baby girl.

I love you Mom
Very much you see,
But when I want to find the woman who gave me
   life
Please feel at ease and assist me.

She gave me life, but you fulfilled it
And none can take your place.
Sure I want to meet her and even be a friend,
And talk to her face to face.

But you have no reason to worry,
You also had help from above.
You also have a special gift,
You have a mother's real love.

Wendy Clements, 15
Marion, Texas

Teenage Years—Troubled Times

Sometimes adoptive parents decide to seek out birthparents when their children are having major problems. They realize the complexities of adolescence, compounded by the voids of closed adoption. Along with parents who are seeking services when their children are faring well, we are also seeing more parents wanting assistance during troubled times. Already facing their children's alienation, they take these steps for the well-being of the children they love. The characteristic these parents share is one of crisis as the problems escalate and solutions seem nowhere in sight. They feel there can only be positive movement. Their children have been involved with self-destructive behavior, including drugs, sexually acting out, running away, and other behaviors leading to dire results.

Michael

When her son was 17 years old, Joanna asked for help in locating her son's birthmother. Michael had been adopted as a toddler and had suffered abuse. Many emotional wounds were still fresh and unhealed. His life lacked direction, and his behavior exhibited the multitude of problems he carried within himself.

Within a short time, his birthmother was found and contact was facilitated. She, too, had lived with emotional wounds, full of guilt for the abuse she had allowed her son to experience. Michael also entered into contact with his paternal grandparents. Through this experience, he gained a clearer sense of self, filling the gaps for the multitude of questions he had. Healing began to take place for all of those involved.

When he and his adoptive parents spoke with the social worker several years later regarding the timing and effects of this contact, they all felt the outcomes were most positive. He was able to use his energy now to confront other issues in his life. His adoption was no longer the mystery it had been. While all his problems were not resolved as the result of the contact, Michael and his parents felt that it contributed to the progress that he was making in his life. His relationship with his birthfamily was loose at best, but that was satisfactory to Michael at this time.

Sarah

Penny and Rog adopted their daughter, Sarah, as an infant. During the growing years, she exhibited no distress pertaining to her adoption. When she was 15, she began having identity problems. She wanted to know who she was, whom she looked like, and where her characteristics came from. All of these problems manifested themselves in deep rebellion towards her parents, moral values, dress, and basic beliefs in God.

The change that came over her seemed sudden to her stunned parents. They sought counseling and other forms of assistance in their local community. None of these made any difference. Feeling a need to remove her from her peers in an effort to break the cycle, they sent her to a residential religious facility. The adolescent who arrived there was a hostile, alienated one. Sarah was resistant to the overtures made to her by those at this residence. Staying there was definitely not her choice. She remained withdrawn, uncommunicative, and despondent.

Her concerned parents continued to seek avenues for helping their child. After a three-month period of residency, the administrator, June Barnard, told them something Sarah had said at one of their group counseling sessions, "She blurted out, 'I don't know who I am and never will!' I picked up on that and asked her if she desired to find her biological mother. She answered, 'Sometimes I do.' I then asked her if she loved the adoptive parents, to which she replied, 'Yes, but they don't understand me. . . . I'm different from them.' "

As the result of this exchange, Penny and Rog sought out a professional intermediary to contact their daughter's birthmother. As June relates:

> . . . Penny and Rog have been, from the beginning, supportive and tenacious about finding the cause and cure of Sarah's dilemma. . . . They asked for my opinion of their attempting to locate Sarah's birthmother. . . . I realized that the results of such a venture could be surprising and far-reaching, indeed, at worst could be damaging to the ultimate reconciliation of this family . . . The hope remained in my heart . . . that this could be the key to Sarah's recovery.

When teens learn that their parents are responding to what is often an unspoken need, they feel validated and understood. Sarah, now 16, in her own words writes:

> The first time I heard my parents had contacted her, I was shocked. My mouth must have dropped ten feet. I wasn't sure quite what to say for fear my parents would feel rejected, although inside I was so excited. I wanted to know everything, but then I wasn't sure, I didn't know what to think, do, or say.

When located, Kathy, Sarah's birthmother, was invited to write Sarah a letter, sharing of herself. Kathy was overjoyed to learn about Sarah, even though these were difficult times. June Barnard writes:

> The day the letter from Sarah's birthmother arrived, I called Sarah to my office and watched her as she read

the words written in a style so similar to her own handwriting. She wept, she smiled, she read the letter again and still again. I saw relief come over her countenance and a light appear in her eyes. I asked Sarah, "How does this make you feel?" She replied. "Happy, very happy!" I asked if she knew why. She said it made her feel normal and like everybody else. Some weeks went by before I spoke with Sarah again about her feelings, but I observed an immediate attitude change. Sarah, who before this had made no attempt to express her emotions, began to laugh, tell jokes, and make friends. A perennial smile developed, and her eyes kept shining. She began to take more interest in school and even to excel. . . . Most importantly of all, the hostility and estrangement between Sarah and her parents just melted away. She can't wait each time for their calls, their letters, and their visits. . . . The discovery of her birthmother seems to have cemented the bonding between Sarah and her parents. Although Sarah looks forward to meeting her birthmother, this doesn't appear to be a great need anymore in her life. It seems enough for Sarah just to know that her birthmother does exist and cares.

The Parents' Perspective

Penny and Rog feel confirmed in their decision to seek out Kathy. They feel fortunate that Sarah has experienced a turning point that is of benefit to her. Penny writes:

We have experienced only positive results knowing. Not knowing brought about all the problems and negatives. . . . We do not feel threatened by the knowledge of Sarah's birthmother. We are just so thankful we were able to find her. . . . We love this woman, too, because without her we would not have a daughter. . . . We anticipate visits back and forth between Sarah and Kathy and would enjoy Kathy and her family visiting us in Texas whenever she is comfortable with that.

During the year following contact, Penny and Rog were sincerely open to including Kathy in their lives. They shared Sarah's joy and did all they could to dispel fears in others whose paths they crossed. They feel they have crossed a bridge in rebuilding the relationship with their daughter. They conveyed how permanent their love was for her and offered continued support and encouragement throughout the stages of contact with Kathy.

Intimacy with their daughter has been regained. They affirm each other as a family. Through their decision to search for Kathy, they, in fact, affirmed themselves, trusting in the relationship they had shared with their daughter for 15 years. Again, bonding and entitlement revisited. As Sarah's parents, they continue to make decisions which they feel are in her best interest.

Sarah's Perspective

When Sarah was asked how she felt about contact with her birthmother, she said:

> First hearing from my birthmother is a feeling that is indescribable. A lot of my questions have been answered. . . . It really excited me to know who I was and am. I still have missing pieces, but I am thankful for what I do know.

About her hopes regarding a relationship with her birthmother, she says, "I see her as a best friend or a future best friend. . . . We have a special bond of love. . . . " Sarah expects that her relationship with her parents will only get closer, "They are and will always be my parents—mom and dad." As far as the timing for this experience, Sarah states:

> I think this was the best time she could have ever come into my life. I needed to know more about my life . . . It helped me so much and has been a big comfort to me. So far, I'm satisfied only to write . . . I would like to see her. I want a relationship with her. But I don't want to rush into anything . . . It was neat to see what Kathy looked like. I see I look a lot like her . . . I was

so excited when I got the packet of pictures, I wanted to take some deep breaths before I could open it. To actually see her was so exhilarating . . . I feel as though I am a complete person.

Sarah wrote the following poem to her birthmother:

CHERISHED CHILD

A mother whose child has
    always been there
Does not comprehend the pain
    a mother must bear
To cherish a child
    then give it away
      In hopes that
        someday
The bond of their hearts
    will string them together
With love tipped darts
    and bring them together
      For a brand new
        start.

On her high school graduation day, surrounded by family and friends, Sarah finally met Kathy. The foundation that was laid through correspondence and telephone exchange contributed to the success of this memorable meeting. Sarah, her parents, and Kathy had many hours to share with one another and to begin a new level of their relationship.

As June writes to the social worker:

The whole story sounds like a fairy tale, and maybe it is if, indeed, fairy tales are merely dreams written on paper. But I do believe it is much more than that. I believe it is proof of a breakthrough in the understanding of the human psyche. I honor your work and consider you a pioneer in the adoptive area of emotional explorations.

From Teenager to Adult—One Story

Laura is an adoptive mom who sought out knowledge about adoption. She realized her three teenage children were dealing with issues for which she had never been prepared. This was largely due to the fact that when she and her husband adopted, there was a limited understanding of adoption.

Her middle daughter, Carolyn, was 16 and demonstrating behaviors that caused her parents grave concern. She had dropped out of school, ran away frequently, and popped back into their lives whenever she needed them to transport or rescue her. Laura and her husband always responded to Carolyn in a loving way. They felt that no matter what, they would be there for her as she journeyed through her troubled adolescence. Laura reported that Carolyn had asked for knowledge of her origins. She had a multitude of questions about her birthmother. As Laura absorbed some knowledge about adoption and intertwined it with her own observations of her children, she became committed to assisting Carolyn.

In spite of the havoc in her daughter's life, Laura evaluated that perhaps knowledge about her birthfamily would help Carolyn find herself. She did not fear losing her to the birthfamily. Laura was thoroughly self-confident of the mother–daughter relationship. She felt that if Carolyn's birthmother was open to contact, she would support Carolyn in this effort.

In recent years there has been an increased understanding of the significance of the running-away pattern of adopted children. They have reported that as a conscious act, they run away looking for birthfamily. Sometimes, the pattern is more subconscious in nature but, nonetheless, connected to this search. Responsive adults are able to assist these youths to identify the underlying issues and possibly reduce the incidence. Again, validation of the need is a critical part of the experience.

Carolyn had the opportunity to voice her need and to be prepared for her search by an adoption professional. She received a summary of the circumstances leading to her adoption. She was also given letters which her birthmother, Janice, had written to the agency inquiring about her welfare after the adoption had taken place. The latter was very confirming for Carolyn in that it concretely conveyed to her the caring that Janice felt for her.

When Janice was located, she was most receptive to including Carolyn and her family in her life. The relationship began through telephone contact and then visits. During the early stages, they had to work on getting acquainted, as their lifestyles had differences. As in any relationship, there were developmental stages that had to be experienced.

Seven years later, Carolyn (now an adult) and Laura report total conviction that the timing for the initial contact was ideal. Laura admits she would not have felt a readiness for this when her children were younger. However, at the point she backed Carolyn in these efforts, she felt secure that this was not going to destroy their relationship. She has found these sentiments to have been correct over time. Laura states that she has no regrets whatsoever, and that Carolyn benefited as she gained a sense of wholeness. She sees the affinity that Carolyn has with her birthfamily. Carolyn herself reports that she is very much like Janice in a multitude of ways—from physical attributes to feelings about a variety of topics.

Laura, with a laugh, recounts that Janice's son was trying to make sense of all the shared interrelationships and asked her if he was another son to her. Whereupon, Laura responded, "Sure!" The family ties are comfortable for all involved. Laura maintains telephone contact with Janice and her parents, as they live in different cities. She feels the bonds with Carolyn have become even stronger as the years have passed.

As Carolyn reflects on the last 7 years, she acknowledges her increased maturity now that she is well into adulthood. She sometimes can't believe the behaviors she exhibited as a teenager. She feels that she met Janice at a good age, so as to make some internal changes. Knowing Janice helped her plan for her own adulthood and relieved her of a multitude of questions.

As she was growing up, Carolyn felt tremendous anger regarding her adoption. She feels that when she learned about the circumstances, it allowed her to let go of the anger. Now she understands and does not have negative feelings for Janice. She identifies Janice as a special friend. Her bonds with Laura are powerful, and she states that no one else can be Mom, nor would she allow that. At the same time, both Carolyn and Laura identify Janice as a "grandma" to Carolyn's children. She has even babysat them for Carolyn when a trip brought them to her area. All in all, the relationship among all these individuals reflects a high comfort level and a commitment to continued contact. Over time their understanding and appreciation of each other has grown and continues to grow. They are investing in a healthier future without secrets.

Adoption triad members and professionals have an obligation to immerse themselves in learning about the essence of the adoption experience of all triad members. When this is done, the natural progression is a responsiveness to self and others. No longer will contact among triad members be questioned or considered pathological. Steps will be actively taken to restore the bonds broken through the closed-adoption system. With understanding comes heightened empathy. With elimination of fear, comes action. Too often the paralysis that grips agencies and adoption triad members has to do with fear and lack of understanding. For those receptive to learning, the information is widely available through reading, conferences, and other forms of personal contact. Adoption, in many respects, is still in the "dark ages." Those who understand have the task to share their knowledge and insight with others.

It behooves adoption professionals and triad members alike to take note of the fact that outreach during the minority years is a beneficial step. It should be a natural intervention, with preparation and support, when needs are expressed. This is the nature of validation. This also takes into account that the roles of adoption triangle members can be cooperative, rather than the traditional adversarial roles.

□ 8 □

OTHER DIMENSIONS OF OPEN ADOPTION

Up to this point, this book has focused on open adoption as it relates to domestic infant adoption, but there are other forms of adoption which can benefit from openness as well. What we have learned about open adoption and its benefits can (and should) be incorporated into other areas of adoption practice. In this chapter we will be discussing openness in adoption within the family (adoption of a relative), foreign adoption, and older children adoption.

In-Family Adoption

In-family adoption has been taking place for centuries, in some cases secretly, while in other cases very openly. In fact, there are countless adult adoptees who have experienced open adoptions by relatives and who can provide insight to help us better understand the long-term impact of open adoption. One such adult adoptee, Andy, told us that he grew up knowing that his aunt was his birthmother, and whenever he wanted to talk with her he could. He further elaborated that his parents were his parents; he did not consider his birthmother to be "Mom." However, Andy considered it very natural and normal to have continued access to his birthmother over the years. This adoptee grew up with openness and honesty, as well as answers to his questions. He did not have any major identity problems, and he was not confused about who his parents were. He simply considered open adoption to be a natural fact of life (in his words "no big deal").

One mother, Lauren, tells us her experience with in-family adoption:

> My husband and I are the proud parents of two wonderful children, Nick, who is 11 and was born to us, and Karisa, who is two years old and was adopted.
>
> Karisa was placed with us at age 7 months, and the adoption was final when she was 9 months old. But our story is special in that we have known and loved her since her birth.
>
> Karisa was born by cesarean section on a warm Sunday evening in June—a most beautiful baby girl. Born to my husband's younger brother, Jon, and his 17-year-old girlfriend, Leia, Karisa is, by blood relation, our niece. We remember clearly the first time we saw her, and from the very beginning of her life we felt an extraordinary love for her.
>
> During Leia's pregnancy, she took excellent care of herself and her unborn baby. Although unplanned, she never considered an abortion. She was determined to lovingly raise her child.
>
> We enjoyed babysitting and often did so during those early months. As summer turned to fall, Leia started back to high school, working towards graduation and making plans to go on to college. During this time she took good care of Karisa—even walking home from school at lunchtime to nurse her.
>
> Karisa was growing and thriving, a healthy, happy baby, but it was becoming increasingly difficult for Leia. Her relationships with Jon and her family were stormy. She was indeed bearing heavy responsibilities for a high school senior.
>
> One day while I was holding Karisa, asleep in my arms, Leia confided to me that it was getting harder for her. And so it was during Karisa's sixth month of life that Leia said to me that she was *considering* adoption. It was becoming clear to her that she was just not ready to be a parent yet—and she wanted a life for Karisa that she simply could not give her now. She told me that she

could never relinquish Karisa to strangers—never knowing where or how she was. Knowing how much we loved her, she was asking us. I told her we would be proud and privileged to raise Karisa.

But Leia needed time to think. I remember taking her hand and looking into her eyes and saying, "Just be *sure*—beyond any doubt. You must be *certain*." She was wrestling with a decision of monumental importance, probably the most important decision she would ever make. Lives would change, forever.

So, while Leia took the time she needed to think out her and Karisa's lives and make a forever decision, we were waiting at home, excited, nervous, and wondering if we would have a daughter.

Late on a Wednesday night in February, Leia came to our home. Tearful and trembling, but yet resolved and strong, she said quietly, "You have a daughter." I held her close and we cried together. Hers were tears of pain, mine were tears of unbelievable joy . . . but together we shared a love for a very special child.

Leia said she would bring Karisa to us the next day. On Thursday, February 6, a snowy, white, winter morning, Leia placed Karisa gently in my arms and said goodbye.

My feelings that day were beyond description. Our wildest dreams—our heart's desire—had been fulfilled in that small pink bundle. That day started our forever together as a family, the four of us.

I know those months before the adoption was final were unbelievably painful for Leia, but showing a maturity far beyond her years, she never wavered.

The legal process of an independent, private adoption is basically the same as that in a "traditional" agency adoption. Both Jon and Leia had to appear in court and voluntarily relinquish their parental rights before we could file a petition to adopt. A homestudy is still required. But on April 18, an unusually warm and fragrant spring day, we happily celebrated Adoption Day. We then had by law what we already had by love, a beautiful baby daughter.

It's been over a year since that snowy day in February when Karisa first came to us. We've been through all four seasons now. Leia has moved away to college, but we keep in touch, and she knows that when she is in town she is welcome to visit. We have talked a lot. She has told us how very much it hurts sometimes, but it's getting easier. She knows where Karisa is, she knows she is happy, healthy, and loved. We have found ourselves in what we have since learned is called "open adoption."

Open adoption is not co-parenting and the adoptive parents are not "babysitters." We are our children's "real" parents. The birthparents generally assume a position similar to that of a distant, but special, friend.

Open adoption is simply another way to build families. Karisa has enriched our lives beyond measure. She is our child. And for us—it's working.

As in Karisa's adoption, there are some unique positives, issues, and complexities when relatives adopt. In these situations, the participants experience all of the benefits which are inherent in any open adoption. In addition, they have the advantage of genetic similarity and continuity because one of the parents has a biological relationship with the child. As Lauren states, "In our case our daughter visibly resembles my husband and son. The paternal side of her 'family tree' is the same, both adoptive and biologically." This can aid the child's sense of "belonging" to the adoptive family, thereby reducing the feeling of being "different." Also, the child has ongoing access to at least one of his birthparents, which provides answers to questions over the years and eliminates the need to search for birthparents.

In-family adoptions are generally done without an intermediary, which means that the important counseling, education, and support previously discussed may be absent in these situations. This has numerous implications—e.g., the birthmother may be more likely to change her mind and take back the child due to the lack of counseling and support, the adoptive parents may feel more threatened and fearful of the birthparents because they have not experienced some education regarding adoption issues, etc. We encourage anyone considering in-family adoption to seek out counseling and educational services, as they are facing the same issues that affect any adoption, plus some additional ones (e.g., adoptive parents must decide how to incorporate the birthparent into the child's life, the type and frequency of contact, etc.).

There is a potential problem in relative adoptions. Even in situations where the adoption has been handled openly and where the related birthparent remains an integral part of the child's life, there can be the tendency to refer to the birth parent as "Aunt Emily" and, somehow, neglect to mention to the child that Emily is also his birthmother. Because "everyone knows," parents can "forget" to be open and honest with the child. It is important in any situation (relative or non-relative) where there is contact or visitation for the parents to be honest with the child from the beginning (and on an ongoing basis) about the birthparent relationship.

Also, in cases where the adoption occurs after the birthparents have already parented the child (as in Karisa's case), there are some unique entitlement issues. As Lauren states, adopting parents "may have a harder time establishing feelings of 'entitlement' to their new child. So many people (friends and relatives) *know* of the situation and it takes time for them to become 'used' to it. We were unnerved several times when people (some we didn't even know!) approached us with 'Oh, *you've* got Leia's baby.' "

Because the adoptive parents continue to relate to the birthparents on a "family" basis, feelings of entitlement usually take longer than in other adoptions. However, this problem is usually only temporary and can be worked through successfully. Open in-family adoption can be a very viable and positive alternative with benefits for all involved, especially the child.

Foreign Adoption

Foreign adoption has become an increasingly popular alternative for prospective adoptive couples, largely because it is frequently a quick avenue to parenthood. There are thousands of children in foreign countries (e.g., Central and South American countries and Asian countries) desperately in need of permanent homes. Typically, these are abandoned infants and older children who are living in orphanages. As a result, there is usually very little information available on the birthparents. However, it is important for us to understand that in some countries abandonment is the only socially acceptable way to place a baby for adoption because of the stigma of an out-of-wedlock pregnancy. Legal relinquishment as we know it may not be the norm. And, in fact, in many of these "abandonment" cases, the foreign adoption agency has information on the birthparents, but, simply because of the stigma, does not pass this information along to the American agency or the adopting couple.

One significant problem in foreign adoption is related to identity issues which adoptees face as the result of the lack of information about their origins. These adoptees may face more identity problems than children adopted domestically because typically there is virtually no information available on the birthparents. (Even in today's closed domestic adoptions there is information about the birthparents which is passed on to the adoptive parents.) Adoptees from foreign countries tell of us the complete void which they experience because of all of the unknowns, because of being uprooted from one culture to another, and because they look different from their adoptive parents. They experience all of the feelings and frustrations that all adoptees experience, except their feelings (e.g., feeling "different") can be magnified because of the unknowns and, in many cases, the very real abandonment. They are angry about the lack of information about themselves. Adolescence is a particularly difficult time for these adoptees as they struggle with the question of "who am I?"

Recently some overseas adoption agencies have become more responsive to requests for information on birthparents and for openness. We encourage adoptive couples to correspond directly with the overseas agency to let them know of their desire for openness, and we have seen many positive results from this approach. In fact, open adoption has become very common in Central and South American countries. Even if there is not the opportunity for open adoption, there can, at least, be some openness (e.g., pictures, letters, etc.).

The letter below demonstrates one mother's attempt to open up communication in a Korean adoption (which typically practices closed adoption and where the stigma regarding an out-of-wedlock pregnancy is very strong). Dawn Holmberg felt compelled to share her story after reading *Dear Birthmother* and, in fact, her request for openness in Korean adoptions may have been one of the first, since she initiated communication with her daughter's birthmother in 1982.

> . . . I am the adoptive mother of a beautiful 2-year-old girl adopted from Korea. As foreign adoption was never mentioned in your book, I wanted to write you as I thought you might be interested in our unique situation in open foreign adoption.
>
> Since the first day our daughter, Jasmine, was placed in our arms (at 10 weeks old) I couldn't shake a feeling that someone in Korea was grieving the loss of this precious child. We decided we wanted to contact her to assure her of Jasmine's well-being. We also were very curious about her and wanted to make contact possible for Jasmine in the future if she chooses this.
>
> We were fortunate to know the name of the birthmother from our referral. We were required to send three progress reports to the Korean agency at 1, 3, and 5 months after placement. With each report we sent a letter to the birthmother and asked that it be translated and forwarded to her, if possible. These reports go first through the American agency and then are sent to Korea.
>
> I was never contacted about our request, so, after several more months, I wrote another letter and sent it directly to a person at the agency who I know, that works with overseas correspondence between the agencies. Jasmine was now over a year old. About a month later they finally called me. They wanted to know our motives in doing this. After we got things settled, they agreed. There was a $150 fee for them to do it, though. It was well

worth the price, as we felt Jasmine's future security might be resting on this. The thought of her ever being plagued by unanswered questions about herself hurts me.

The Korean agency was able to locate her and we received a letter after about three months.

All of our family and friends were very skeptical (to say the least) about our doing this. My mother's first reaction was, "She's ours now, don't do anything to jeopardize that." We found the four myths to be alive and well!

Now that our families have seen the letters and know our feelings better they think it's wonderful and beautiful. We all feel (my mom included) a special closeness to this woman so far away.

I have sent her a photo album with pictures of Jasmine at every month since we've had her. She sent Jasmine a beautiful Korean dress. . . .

We plan to adopt again in the near future and we are requesting a child(ren)—(we may get siblings!)—with a possibility of contact with the birthmother. (Many referrals have no information on this as many babies are left on doorsteps or the mother refuses to reveal her identity.)

I have enclosed copies of our correspondence so far with Jasmine's birthmother. They give a real feeling of peace, both now and for the future. . . .

I wanted to let you know that *open foreign adoption* is possible, too.

The following are the first letters exchanged between the Holmbergs and their birthmother:

Dear Choi Young Sook,

My husband and I are the adoptive parents of your child. We would very much like to have contact with you and write to each other.

We love your child very much. She has brought joy to our home. She will always be told that her birthmother was a good woman in a difficult situation. I am sure she would want to know who you are and maybe we could travel to Korea and meet you some day when she grows up.

Please write to us and send a picture of yourself. We care about you very much. There are so many things we would like to know about you, and our daughter will want to know also.

> *With love,*
> *The adoptive mother*

The letters below from the birthmother are in broken English, due to the translation done in Korea of her letters:

Hello,

I don't know how to thank you for sending me the letter and photo.

My eyes filled with tears when I saw the well grown up children, and I am very happy.

I feel guilty and embarrassed constantly.

I thank you for raising the children with such dedication and love. There is a saying that love for raising the children is thicker than borning the children.

I will always pray for your beautiful dreams of raising the children in the future.

One thing I'd like to ask you is that I'd appreciate very much if you'd write the child's name and the height and weight. Also I can't ask for more if you'd not worry about her future and don't stop the letters and please continue to write. I will thank you if you'd write and send photos again. I wish to meet you someday soon and wish your family luck.

> *Good Bye*
> *Choi, Young Sook*

P.S. I promise to send you a photo of myself in the next letter.

Dear Choi, Young Sook,

We were so glad to get your letter. I have so often thought of you, though I didn't know who you were and wondered how you are and what you are like.

I feel very sad for the painful experience you have had and must live with. Please know that we love our little girl with all our hearts and are grateful to you every day.

Her name is Jasmine Valee Mee Sun Holmberg—

Jasmine: a flower and spice and we think it is a pretty sounding name.

Valee: a middle name my great-grandmother made up. My grandmother, my mother and I also have this name.

Mee Sun: the name she was given in Korea before she came to us, meaning beautiful and good (which she is).

Holmberg: our family name

This is a record of her growth . . . [the chart of height and weight from birth to 17 months, which the Holmbergs sent to the birthmother].

She has had all her shots and is very healthy.

Jasmine started crawling at 10 months and walked at 11 months. Now she can run and dance and climb. She loves other kids, especially her cousins. She is very friendly and waves and says "hi" to everyone when we go out.

She gives hugs and kisses, loves to have books read to her, loves to play chasing and hiding games, playing outside and going on outings.

She says just a few words—"hi," "bye," "Dad," "hot," "no," but understands everything. She is usually happy to obey requests such as "go get your shoes," or "put that back."

About ourselves, when you write us please just call us Tom and Dawn. What should we call you? I think we are very close in age. I was born 6-7-56. What is your birth date? Tom is 9-17-55.

I have 2 brothers, ages 22, single, and in college, and 28 and just married, and a sister, 18, also in college. I went to college for 2 years and got married at 21. I am the only one with a child in my family.

I babysit a 10-month-old girl 2 days a week and just take care of Jasmine the rest of the time. She keeps me busy. I'm glad I don't have to work and can be home with her.

Tom works for his father who owns a printing company. He has three sisters, ages 31, with 1 child, 34, with 2 children, and 38, with 4 children. He is the youngest and only son.

We have been married for 6 years. I have had 2 pregnancies, but both grew in the tube and had to be removed by surgery. I was depressed, but then we thought of adopting and I had hope again. American babies take a long time to get (about

5-10 years) because there are so few available. We learned that we could get a baby from Korea in less than a year, so we decided that was what we wanted. We waited only 7 months for Jasmine. We got our first picture of her at 4 weeks old on May 25 and she came to us on June 25 at just 10 weeks.

About 40 friends and relatives came to the airport to see her come. Everyone was laughing and crying. We were so happy. Five other Korean babies came on the plane, too, and their families were all there waiting for their babies, too.

We are of the Christian faith and attend church on Sundays. Most of our friends are people from church. Our Christian faith is very important to us.

I am curious about you. I hope you don't think I'm rude if I ask some questions about you.

What are your interests and beliefs?

What are your hopes or plans for the future?

How tall are you?

Were you able to stay with your baby for a while after she was born?

Does the father know what happened?

Please ask us any questions you have. We will be happy to tell you anything you want to know.

We wish you peace and happiness.

Love,
Dawn Holmberg

Dear Mr. and Mrs. Holmberg,

One's mind is apt to wander when spring comes. We call the wind in spring "Kkot Sam Wind," which means that the winter is jealous of the spring and makes the wind blow so that the flower might not blossom.

How are you, Mr. and Mrs. Holmberg? I believe Jasmine has grown up beautifully. It is a great pleasure to receive a letter with photos of her. As I see her in pictures, my eyes fill with tears because of yearning for her. I can't find suitable words to express my deep gratitude for your excellent care and love to her. My anxiety about her is disappeared thoroughly, as I received your letter. I think Jasmine has a very nice family, and thank you again very deeply.

Today, I would like to give a small gift to her in remembrance of her second birthday. It is a Korean dress. I hope it fits well to her. It will be greatly appreciated if you take a picture of her wearing this dress, and send it to me.

Now, I would like to introduce myself. I was born June 15, 1959, as the second daughter of four sisters and two brothers. My younger brothers and sisters are attending school. I liked painting in school days and was able to play volleyball, ping pong, and tennis. My height is 160 cm and weight is 50 kg.

My future plan is to live alone and manage a small book store. I thought about marriage before, but now have no intention to marry. Our country has many differences with yours in social morality and custom. I don't believe in God now. Someday, I might turn to God. In this situation, my only hope is that Jasmine grow up as a wonderful girl.

I referred her to adoption agency without seeing her face as soon as I have her. So, I always imagine how she is. My heart filled with joy and happiness as I found her figure in her pictures. I will always pray God for you and your family. Jasmine is now your own daughter. Please bring her up as a charming and nice girl. And I will send my photos next time, if you want.

I hope you are always in the best of health and spirit.

With my best wishes,
Sincerely yours,
Choi, Young Sook

These letters were pioneering ones in terms of openness in foreign adoption, but many families have followed in the Holmberg's footsteps, making open adoption and semi-open adoption a reality in foreign adoption.

Older Children Adoption

The principles which we have discussed in terms of open adoption also apply to older children or special needs adoption. In fact, there may even be a stronger need for open adoption in the placement of older children because these children have been parented by their birthparents and have a relationship with these parents, as well as vivid memories. It is unrealistic to expect a child of age 3 or 10 to simply "forget" his birthparents and to pretend he was "born" on the day of his adoptive placement (which is what traditional adoption agencies have attempted to accomplish). Even if his parents have been abusive and if he cannot return to live with them, he can still maintain a relationship with them.

Frequently, adoption social workers are opposed to open adoption in older children placements because of the birthparents' history and problems. Obviously, if a child's life would be in jeopardy, open adoption would not be appropriate (although openness might). However, most situations are not this extreme. The fact that the birthparent has problems (e.g., drug usage) does not justify cutting all ties with the child. In fact, an older child's chance of success in an adoptive placement can be enhanced by allowing contact to be maintained with the birth family, thereby reducing the child's need to disrupt the placement in order to return to the birthparents (frequently a fantasy) or reestablish contact with them.

Actually, in recent years, open adoption has become a popular compromise in legally contested cases. Some lawyers advise birthparents who are fighting to regain custody of their children to agree to a settlement which provides for open adoption with limited visitation because, if they lose the court fight, the child is likely to be placed in a closed adoption, where parental contact is permanently lost. One birthmother said, "If I had fought all the way through and lost, my rights would have been completely terminated. I would have never been able to see my kids again. It would have been just like they died." Instead, this birthmother decided that it would be in the children's and her best interest for them to be placed for adoption and for her to have visitation rights every six months. While open adoption should not be used as a tool to terminate birthparents rights when that is not in the child's best interest, it is important to offer open adoption to children and parents who must be separated because it allows the relationship to continue, rather than to be completely severed. It acknowledges the child's past, rather than denies it. And it allows the child to care for both sets of parents.

The following letter from an adoptive mom demonstrates one family's experience with open older child (age 12 at the time of placement) adoption:

> A few months after the placement, Cindi's social worker arranged for her to have a "termination" visit with her birthmother. This woman, whom I'll call Gail, had placed her daughter in foster care after discovering she had been sexually abused by her stepfather. Cindi had previously spent over a year in foster homes because of sexual abuse by her biological father, Gail's first husband. Gail apparently felt she could not protect Cindi from further sexual abuse. She was not prepared to leave her second husband. Gail relinquished parental rights after Cindi had been in foster care for the second time for nearly a year. There had been no visits between them for a long time before the relinquishment and none afterwards.
>
> So our new daughter's social worker convinced us of the need to have a "good-bye" visit, to allow Cindi to finally hear from her own mother the reasons why she was given up for adoption. The social worker also tried to arrange such a visit with Cindi's birthfather, who had relinquished her out of fear of prosecution for the prior sexual abuse. He refused to cooperate.
>
> The termination visit took place in the small town where the birthmom lived, some 40 miles from our home. Gail said all the right things with the help of the social worker. She assured Cindi that she loved her and that it was her own problems at the time that caused her to give Cindi up for adoption. She had since separated from her second husband, but she was able to admit that she did not feel she could protect Cindi from future abuse. She and Cindi cried and embraced. The whole thing went so well that when Gail asked me if she could write to Cindi occasionally, I consented. Cindi's brother and half sister were still at home with her birthmother, and Cindi worried and wondered about them a great deal. I realized that I didn't really know what I was getting into, but it seemed

like the natural and right thing to do. On the drive home from the visit, Cindi confessed that "I always thought my mother didn't love me." Her elated mood convinced me that the visit had been a very positive experience for her.

In the months that followed, Gail wrote regularly. Her letters were supportive and full of news of Cindi's siblings and her own adventures. They were a source of pride and joy to Cindi. My husband and I agreed to allow a second visit about six months after the first. I had spoken to Gail by phone several times and sensed that she could continue to be a positive factor in Cindi's life.

Gradually, as our trust of Gail increased and as Cindi grew older and more capable of protecting herself, the visits between her and her birthmother increased. The first overnight visit was a scary experience for my husband and me. It took place over the Christmas holidays, and we called Cindi at her birthmother's home the second day to reassure her of our love. We weren't sure that she'd be willing to return home with us after the weekend, but she was. She seemed as ready to leave as she had been to come.

Eventually we settled into a routine of 4-5 day visits twice a year, during summer and Christmas holidays. Cindi and her birthmother had trouble getting along sometimes, as they had before the separation. They each appeared to be satisfied with the twice-yearly visits and unlimited correspondence, and neither pushed for more. Cindi never tried to run away, no matter how angry she became with us. I guess there was no need: She knew exactly what life was like at her birthmother's home. The regular visits prevented Cindi from harboring many fantasies. I felt this freed her to concentrate on the hard work of growing up in a new family.

I remember one occasion when, angry with her behavior, we threatened to cancel Cindi's visit with her birthmom. Cindi angrily reminded us that "You may be my legal parents, but they are still my family!" Her words stung, as did her constant reference to Gail as her "real" mom. But these comments helped us keep in touch with reality. We were the last of a long line of substitute families for Cindi; she was "ours" only so long as we accepted all of her past, previous moms included.

Through our shared arrangement, Cindi got to watch her biological brother and sister grow up. She attended her biological grandmother's funeral. She watched first-hand her birthmother's successful efforts to locate her own younger brothers (Cindi's uncles), who had been given up for adoption as infants. She was able to maintain a sense of belonging to the family of her origin, where she had spent the first 10 years of her life. I am grateful that her birthmother was able to be so supportive of Cindi, and of our roles, after the traumatic events that separated them.

When Cindi turned 18 she fulfilled a long-cherished wish and moved in with her birthmother. After a few months she moved out again because they couldn't get along, but this time it was Cindi's choice to leave. Cindi is now in the military and is struggling with problems typical of adolescents. She is doing a pretty good job of it, and we are proud of her. Her families are still very important to her. She calls faithfully and divides her precious leave time between her homes. This past Thanksgiving she brought her biological sister to our home to share in our son's second birthday party. As I scrubbed dishes after dinner, Cindi's little sister put her arm around my waist and gave me a big hug. It felt real good. Somehow our crazy adoption arrangement worked, and I believe we all benefited from it.

This powerful story reinforces that we must continue to look for opportunities for openness and honesty in all forms of adoption.

□ 9 □

LONG-TERM BENEFITS FOR EVERYBODY

The problems which are inherent in traditional, closed adoption have been well documented and led to the evolution of open adoption. As we have discussed throughout this book, there are definite benefits for all parties in open adoption. However, as we have also learned, there is no "perfect" adoption. There can be problems or complexities in any adoption because adoption involves extra issues and differences from biological parenthood. But the secrecy and shame associated with traditional adoption have been replaced with honesty and openness, resulting in a healthier experience for everyone.

One of the most significant benefits in open adoption is that the adopting parents and birthparents are completely in control and in charge of the adoption experience, rather than the control being in the hands of agencies or other intermediaries. Birthparents and adopting parents make all of their own decisions and determine how the adoption experience will go for them, instead of agencies telling them how it will be. As in other areas of life, people fare better when they are in control of their own lives and making their own decisions. In addition, adopted children are the primary beneficiaries of open adoption, as it enables them to grow up in an atmosphere of honesty and openness (which is important for *any* child).

Normalization of Adoption

Bruce M. Rappaport in "The Normalization of Adoption" refers to open adoption as "normalized" adoption:

... We prefer to call the process *"normalized"* adoption rather than "open" adoption. The distinction is critical. In an open and democratic society like ours, open and aboveboard procedures should be the norm, and closed, secretive operations should be the exception. If our adoption procedures seem so radical, it is only because adoption has been a totally closed process for so long that somehow it has become "normal" to build a family in secrecy and "unusual" to want to do it openly. . . .

Open adoption is an attempt to recreate that special quality of having your child adopted within your own family. The birthmother (and father) are able to have their child adopted . . . by somebody . . . with whom they have established a very powerful relationship.

There needs to be a recognition that there are some new and difficult relationships to work out and, for that reason, that solid support and professional counseling are critical to the process. . . .

The concept of the normalization of adoption acknowledges open adoption as a healthier, more positive experience, and, in effect, a more *normal* process, compared to traditional adoption which must no longer be viewed as an acceptable form of adoption practice. This concept also incorporates our new definitions of open adoption and the new family relationship (Chapter 1) in recognizing the birthparents as relatives/extended family members. If the adoptive parents accept the birthparents as relatives, then it becomes very natural to include them in the child's life over the years. This leads to a positive and *normalized* adoption experience.

Benefits for Adoptive Parents

In addition to normalizing adoption and allowing adoptive parents to be in control of their lives, open adoption enables adoptive parents to lose their feelings of fear and threat. They are also given "permission" to parent and a real sense of entitlement to their children.

Laurie Morkert, an adoptive mother, comments on the benefits for her husband and herself:

> We know our children's birthparents, and we know what a loving and painful decision it was for them to place their children with us. We have information from Ann and Lee (birthmothers) that we can share with the children as they grow, and we can share information with others. Openness gives you permission to be able to share the circumstances behind your child's arrival, if you choose to do so.

Laurie adds that she has never felt threatened by her children's birthmothers because "We can never have too many people love us, and our children are lucky that so many people love them."

Judy Albrecht describes the benefits for herself as a parent:

> Open adoption brings adoption to the fore in a healthful, natural context . . . or, at least, that has been my experience. Rather than reduce the sense of belonging, openness has merely helped establish my daughter's status—"as is," not "as if." By endorsing her totality— which includes her original family—she belongs *more* to our family than if we had denied or rejected that reality.
>
> I have a sense of unity and balance because I have dealt with my connectedness to Katherine (birthmother). I am not anxious or fearful of her. I can parent "in toto"— not in avoidance or denial.
>
> I can deal with the community as an adoptive parent. I am different, not intensely so, but, at least, on an awareness level. By working through and acknowledging the differences (Kirk, *Adoptive Kinship*), I have become *more* entitled and less ambiguous in the concrete "light of day" and the ongoingness of adoption kinship and Katherine.
>
> I am more sensitive to others through my empathy with my child's birthparent. I have greater intuition for grief in every context not just adoption.

I also have more energy for myself and my role as a parent because I don't have to expend psychic energy suppressing conflicts over issues of my adoptive parent status or my infertility.

It has brought us closer together as a family to face ourselves and to grow together.

Missy Mial also describes the benefits for herself:

For me I think the most important benefit is that I really feel like I know my children. I have the same advantage that biological parents have. I can attribute their strengths, weaknesses, quirks, and looks to a real person whom I've touched, talked to and laughed with. I can't imagine not being able to do this! It's wonderful to know firsthand why they look the way they do, sound the way they do, and even, in many instances, act the way they do. Knowing them this well allows me to be a more complete parent. With the information I have and the future contact we expect to have with Sherry, I am convinced that I will be able to help my children through their difficult years of identity searching. Also, there is, of course, medical information that is available to us that we would not otherwise have. Last, but not least, there is the peace of mind for me that their birthmother was, and is, comfortable with the decision she made. This is extremely important to me.

Michael and Robbie Archer add:

The benefits of open adoption have been invaluable. We have gotten information about our daughters' backgrounds which might have been lost forever if we had not been in contact with their birthparents. Haley and Tyler both know who they look like—Haley has her birthmother's beautiful brown hair, brown eyes, and smooth, dark complexion, and Tyler has her birthmother's beautiful blonde hair, green eyes, and fair (but dry) skin. We are also aware of any health problems they may face now or in the future.

Knowing Haley's and Tyler's birthparents has not only given us information, but a peace of mind which comes from knowing that we will not go through life looking at everyone we meet and wondering if that person is our child's birthmother or birthfather. Additionally, knowing the birthparents so well and that they would never do anything to disrupt their childrens' lives, has kept us from ever feeling threatened.

Becca Marsh describes the ongoing relationship which her family has experienced:

It seemed a very natural and comfortable thing to do. We have had no reason to regret it. We exchange letters and cards throughout the year. They usually come to our house around Christmas and then again around Robbie's birthday. They have spent the night with us three times. They have never brought a gift for Robbie without also bringing one for our older son. I appreciate this thoughtfulness from them. I send them pictures of both boys, and they have sent pictures of themselves as children, as well as current pictures of their siblings. It's so neat to see different resemblances in facial expressions, as well as in physical features. We enjoy seeing who Robbie looks like and where his personality originated. We call sometimes if we have not heard from each other through the mail for an extended period of time.

We still feel very comfortable with so much openness. And we have told the birthparents that we anticipate to always communicate with them. A fringe benefit for us has been that we now have two special friends that we enjoy being with. It is so neat to have someone to tell about all the wonderful things your child does and to know that they think he is truly amazing, too!

Jeanne Etter, who has been involved in ongoing visitation for eleven years, sees clear benefits in open adoption:

The intangibles are that we know our child's heritage. We all know that the adoption happened because it was what everyone wanted. Our child knows that she came to us in love. Her birth relatives have never stopped caring for her anymore than we do. If some problem arises in the teen years, we have all our years of working together to plan what is best for Angela. We never have to fear a stranger on our doorstep or a teenager running away to an unknown place to look for a missing piece of herself. Cooperation is really all it takes, and because of the love involved it's a pleasure, not a chore.

Phylis Speedlin observes that a major benefit has been how comfortably her children have processed their adoption experiences. She relates that the girls cannot understand why the public has such an interest in open adoption. "Why is anyone interested?" they ask. To them, it is normal and not a big deal. The intensity of the closed adoption experience has given way to a natural flow of interaction through open adoption.

Benefits for Birthparents

As we have discussed, in open adoption birthparents work through the normal feelings of grief in a healthier manner, and they are more at peace with their decision. Being active in the child's life helps them each time feelings of grief resurface at different stages.

Debbie Scannell, who engages in ongoing visitation, shares her feelings of peace six years after placement:

> . . . In the six years since her birth, I have fulfilled many of my own dreams. I completed nursing school, met and married a wonderful man, travelled six months in Europe, and most recently have given birth to a wonderful baby boy. It's a lot different now knowing I'm ready to be a mother. One thing is for sure—if I knew then what I know now about all that is involved in motherhood, there would have been no question about the adoption. My feelings toward my firstborn haven't changed—in fact, I find it even more important to keep up good contact, as I don't want her to feel she's been replaced.
>
> I am very happy with my decision and the direction

the adoption has taken. The open communication is great, and I look forward to future visits.

Tina, a birthmother of an eight-year-old, comments on her feelings regarding ongoing visitation:

I only get to see her about once a year (because the adoptive family presently lives out of the country), but that is so helpful. I also get letters and pictures on a regular basis. I know who my daughter is, and she knows me. She has already asked a few questions, and I've been there to answer them. And I want her to know that I will always be there if and when she needs me.

Another birthmother, Deirdre Patillo, shares her experiences with open adoption, including visitation, four years after the adoption:

I think that openness has had a wonderful effect on my daughter, her family, and me. My decision for adoption was, of course, emotionally difficult, but I felt, and feel, that it was the most practical and logical decision I have ever made. I don't make snap decisions, and my adoption choice was well-thought out and weighed against other options. Because I was very young, I felt that I was not ready to parent at all, much less to parent alone. The availability of contact with my daughter's parents before and after placement made my choice easier and convinced me of the validity of this choice for my child.

My relationship with Tyler and her family consists mainly of phone calls and visits. Because we live in the same city and because I am an extraordinarily lazy (and illegible) correspondent, this seems to work out best for us. I do try to remember to give Tyler a card or letter at least on her birthday, so she will have some concrete evidence of my love. Of course, at her age the most significant proof of love for her are gifts, pictures, and visits, but, whenever I see her, I do try to reinforce these with the message that I love her. Her parents are wonderful about consistently affirming, both for Tyler and Haley, the love of all members of all the families.

The role I play in Tyler's life is very much that of an extended family member. Tyler and Haley respond to my visits just as they would an aunt or close cousin coming to visit, especially one who brings gifts. Tyler calls me "Deirdre" or "birthmother" or a combination of these. Before she could enunciate well, she called me "Adra Burtmudder"—which I think is cute. I guess the role which I play for Tyler, which makes me feel best about openness, is as a provider of psycho/social historical background. Besides biological traits like similar features, dry skin, and chunkiness, she and my family share similar character traits, habits, and talents. My family is very musical, and Tyler is already exhibiting a propensity for music. A good example is that when I was small (so my siblings tell me), I had an exceptional memory for song lyrics and sang on key from a very early age. My niece, Casey, and Tyler both share this ability, as well. But the strangest coincidence is that Casey (1½ years older) and Tyler make up very similar songs. As a matter of fact, they both have songs which they call their "blues." They also share a temperament!

There were a number of things which were important to me when I made my adoption decision that I would not have known about had I not been given the opportunity to communicate with my daughter and her family. For instance, I really hoped to place Tyler in a family with other children. The fact that Robbie and Michael had already adopted Haley endeared them to me. It was not only the simple fact that they had a child, but the manner in which they spoke of her and her joyous countenance were evidence for me that theirs was an extremely nurturing and happy home. Just knowing Robbie and Michael has made me confident that I made the best decision for Tyler. Also, knowing them has been great for me as a person. Robbie and Michael have always validated my emotions and made me feel worthwhile as a person, aside from my role as a birthmother. They have been extremely important to my development. When I met them before Tyler's birth, they assured me that whatever decision I made would be valid, and they felt I was competent and caring in my choice. They were also extremely considerate and helpful to me during the very difficult time after placement. I know that without their assurance of love and support my period of grieving would have been far more painful, rather than the cathartic growing experience which it turned out to be.

Robbie, Michael, Haley, and, especially, Tyler are four of the greatest people I know and my best friends.

Benefits for Extended Family Members

There are also benefits in open adoption for extended family members, particularly those whose only familiarity with adoption has been closed adoption, with all of its inherent negative stereotypes. Extended family members (especially older generations) are typically "scared" of open adoption when they first hear of the concept, mostly because of these stereotypes and because they fear that their children may "lose" the adopted child. Family members typically still believe in all of the myths and have not had the benefit of the educational process which the adoptive parents have experienced. Adoptive parents must take on the task themselves of educating their families. Encouraging them to read adoption books helps, as well as continuing to share with them over time the experience of open adoption.

One adoptive mother relates her family's fears about open adoption:

My parents and my husband's parents all feel the same way about open adoption. They do not trust it, and they think we are totally crazy to be involved with it. They are very scared that ultimately *their* children (my husband and I) will be hurt by all of this. We have tried to explain it to them from all angles, but they still think of adoption as it was when they were young parents and some

of their friends adopted children. I guess what I am trying to say is they are still living in the cave days in regards
to adoption.

June Taubert Walker, an adoptive grandmother, describes
her initial feelings of apprehension and her own evolution as
the result of her son's and daughter-in-law's experience with
open adoption:

> My reaction to the news was so mixed. . . . I was
> glad, I was happy, I was anxious, I was concerned, and,
> yet, somehow confident. Glad, because I knew how much
> they had wanted a child. Happy because I was going to
> be a grandmother. Proud because I knew they would be
> wonderful parents. Anxious because I had not heard of
> "open adoption" and, after I learned what it meant, I
> wondered how they could do this, and still feel comfort-
> able. And concerned because I felt they deserved a life
> not complicated by a birthmother who could change her
> mind and want her baby back. And, at the same time, con-
> fident because these two were intelligent, sensitive, realis-
> tic people who had made a decision they felt was suited
> to them.
>
> And now some three years have gone by, and it is
> just as they said it would be. Although the birthmother
> has been to visit the child she gave to Jim and Berta, she,
> nonetheless, has gone on to finish college, get married,
> and lead a life of her own with the knowledge that her
> decision not to have an abortion, while it didn't neces-
> sarily benefit her, definitely brought a boundless amount
> of joy that has touched numerous people—likened to a
> stone tossed into the water—the ripples going on and on
> indefinitely, and it showed me that any concerns I might
> have had were needless, and this truly was the best of
> all worlds.

Laurie Morkert notes that she and her husband, Craig,
visited with one of their birthmothers during the time that
Craig's parents also happened to be visiting. The visit with the
birthmother was not held at their home because they "thought

Craig's dad wouldn't be able to handle meeting Lee, as adoptions were done so differently in 'his' day (1940's). Later his dad said that he regretted not having been able to meet Lee. This is the same man who thought (when Cara was a baby) that we shouldn't even tell her she was adopted!''

Laurie also recalls a conversation between her father and a friend of his as they were driving her to the airport. Laurie's dad explained to his friend, "Laurie and Craig got to meet with Daniel's birthmother." Laurie adds, "I think this is terrific! Both of these men are 73 years old and are extremely conservative men—I think our being comfortable with openness has allowed them to feel comfortable with it as well."

Benefits for Adoption Professionals

Adoption professionals are not part of the adoption triangle, yet they are a vital part of the adoption experience. They can facilitate a positive, healthy open adoption experience, or they can take "control" of the process, thereby giving the adoption participants the message that they do not have the ability to make decisions for themselves. We prefer to view adoption as a healthy process in which the adopting parents and birthparents are capable of making, and, in fact, fare better if they do make all of the decisions in adoption. This is, after all, *their* adoption, not ours.

Some social workers have difficulty letting go of the control and power involved in agency practice. They have gotten used to making decisions for people, and they like doing so. They may feel that they have the "professional expertise" to make the *best* decisions for people. In fact, many social workers around the country have told us that, while they like the concept of openness, they do not want to relinquish the power to decide who gets the baby. Some have asked, "Can we offer open adoption without letting the birthmother pick the family?" In open adoption, it is *essential* for social workers to let go of this control and allow their clients to take control of their own destiny. So adoption professionals must be able to look at their own "control" issues and to learn from the well documented problems in traditional adoption in order to be able to facilitate healthier adoptions.

After letting go of the power and control, adoption professionals have different but equally important roles, with clear benefits for them, as well. In open adoption, the adoption professional facilitates the adoption process, provides counseling and support services, as well as educational services to prepare his clients for the unique issues and realities involved in adoption. In fact, his most important role is to see that adopting parents are educated and prepared to deal with adoption over the years. In assuming these new and very important roles, the adoption professional is free from the burden and responsibility of making decisions for other people's lives. For example, he does not have the burden of trying to find a 'perfect' family for the birthparents or deciding how much information about the birthparents to share with the adopting parents. Instead, he assumes the role of a *helping* professional, and this actually feels better than the controlling role.

In traditional adoption, many adoption professionals—in witnessing the grief, loss, and other complexities of adoption—go through stages of being opposed to adoption as a practice. With openness, all of these issues are not eliminated, but avenues are available to better handle them. Professionals can offer their expertise in helping those involved navigate these complexities. By having all parties available, issues can be confronted and dealt with.

Debra Parelskin is an adoption counselor who worked for 10 years in traditional adoption before making the change to open adoption. She describes her feelings about both forms of adoption, as well as the benefits which she has experienced in open adoption:

> I was surprised at how easy a transition it was from traditional adoption counselor to "open adoption" counselor. I always felt an uneasiness with the fragmentation of the closed adoption process. On the one hand I worked with the birthmother and witnessed her profound sadness in working through her decision, where her only choices were to keep the baby or place with strangers.

Then on the other hand, I worked with the anxious adoptive couple who trusted that one day I would place the perfect baby with them so they could live happily ever after. Birthparents never saw the joy their gift of life brought the couple and which could have eased their pain. And the adoptive parents had great difficulty empathizing with the birthparents' situation and the difficulty of their decision. Their lives only connected through me and how I presented their stories to one another. There was never a natural flow to the process.

Frankly, the transition to open adoption was a relief. I was tired of "playing God" and deciding who got the few babies available. I recall when I would pick a baby up from the hospital and deliver it to the happy couple that *I* was "placed on a pedestal" and sent flowers, rather than the birthmother. And I still receive the yearly cards and photos during the holidays that I wish could be shared with the birthparents.

Adoption should be recognized as a continuous and lifelong process where everyone is real to one another. There are no longer hidden secrets and great fears of running into each other one day. This negative energy has become positive and constructive energy. Couples utilize their own problem-solving skills in helping birthparents overcome their difficulties.

As a counselor I am now part of the team. I facilitate the meeting between birthparents and adoptive parents and offer them support and encouragement. I provide counseling and resources to help them reach their goals.

The relationship between the birthparents and adoptive parents can be likened to a marriage. They have chosen one another, and I never interfere or stop the match. If problems arise I can facilitate better communication so they are prepared to handle any differences that may arise in the future.

What seems most significant to me in open adoption (again like a marriage) is the foundation of trust that develops. Everyone's future is built on trust.

Benefits for Children

We have intentionally saved the children for the last section of this chapter; they are the focal point of the whole adoption experience, and they are the ones who most directly benefit from the openness in which their birthparents and adoptive parents have participated. As we have discussed throughout this book, in open adoption children have access to ongoing and accurate information about their birthparents and, in effect, themselves. This allows them to feel positive about themselves and about adoption. As a result, these children demonstrate positive self-esteem, compared to the sense of rejection and poor self-esteem frequently characteristic of children with traditional adoptions.

Laurie Morkert describes what she perceives as the benefits for her daughter, age 8:

> Cara will know she doesn't have to be embarrassed by the word *adopted*. She knows what it means, and she is proud of it. She has even brought the picture of Ann (her birthmother) to school for show and tell! Although I don't think that it will always be easy for her as she continues to grow, I am relieved that we will be able to say, "Yes, your birthmother did love you" (in response to such statements as "your birthmother didn't love you."). We have her words written right here.

Laurie further comments:

> Although we have received only about 8 letters from Ann over the past 4 years, we were truly able to see her growth as a person during that period of time, and we were also able to get at least a glimpse of her personality. This has allowed us to witness how Cara's personality is like Ann's. For example, Ann thinks things over carefully and so does Cara. Both also *love* dogs and sports. Both also tend to be very serious and like to have lots of activity in their lives. Also, as Cara's penmanship is becoming clearer, I think her handwriting is going to resemble Ann's. I remember mentioning this to Cara's pediatrician once,

and he thought that was something very positive about openness—that the adoptee got to see how they were like their birthparents.

Missy Mial describes the benefits for her two children who are brothers by birth as well as adoption:

> My children are boys, ages 6 and 8. They both know that they were adopted and have met their birthmother. There are many pictures in our family album of her with us on placement day and on subsequent outings over the years. We have video tapes of us all together. We talk about her a lot. My eight-year-old rarely says anything about her or asks questions. This, however, is very typical of his personality. His little brother, on the other hand, asks questions such as, "You are not my real mother, right?" or "Who nursed me when I was in the hospital?" Usually he is looking for assurance from me that I am his "real" mother and always will be. Always the questions lead to a discussion on the differences between mother and birthmother. These questions are typical of this age.
>
> It would be impossible for me to satisfy my childrens' curiosity about their adoptions without the insight and knowledge that I have as a result of open adoption. I feel it will give them something that is their birthright—an understanding of the woman responsible for their births and a knowledge of their heritage. The wealth of information available to them as they grow up and the healthy attitudes regarding their adoptions will be extremely important to their well-beings, particularly their self-esteem.

Michael and Robbie Archer also see benefits for their two daughters:

> They know, firsthand, why they were placed for adoption and that their birthparents' decisions were made purely out of love and concern for each of them. Most important of all, they know that their birthparents still love them, and they have grown to know and love their birthparents.

Barbara Clark adds:

> The benefits of openness have been Bree (10 years old) feeling more complete about himself. Most of his questions about his adoption have been answered, mainly the "why?" He *really knows* his birthparents are fine people but that they were not ready to parent when he was born. He knows he didn't do anything wrong and that they were not ready to parent *any* child, not just him.
>
> I feel, as he reaches the difficult adolescent years, it will be easier for him because he will not be consumed with questions about his adoption and birthparents.

Ongoing Contact and Intimacy

Ongoing contact provides an avenue for the seeds to develop regarding love, permanence, and trust. In closed adoption, children do not have avenues for obtaining concrete evidence of these ingredients. This affects their ability to love themselves and have trust in their world. Large numbers of adoptees have severe problems in the area of establishing bonds of intimacy. Having experienced an original loss—the loss of the first parents—trust in relationships and their permanence is shaken and difficult to develop.

Children having the opportunity to have contact with birthparents grow up hearing that they are loved. Birthparents are able to be part of their permanent and, therefore, trusted circle. These children grow up with knowledge and feelings whose origin may not be remembered and yet be firmly implanted in their being. They *know*. This, in turn, affects their capacity to form intimate bonds with others, both within their adoptive family and birthfamily, as well as others outside this group.

As trust and intimacy develop, bonding is also affected. We have observed tighter bonding between children and their parents the more freed up these children are to process their adoption reality. What could be more desirable than the ability to bond within intimate relationships.

Openness and Individuation

A further outcome of open adoption is that for children to feel secure individuating, they must feel secure in those parents from whom they must individuate. As children get confirmation that they were and are loved by both sets of parents, the issues of abandonment and rejection recede in intensity. Individuation then becomes possible.

These issues are prominent ones in closed adoption. Adult adoptees often speak of the fact that since they lost one set of parents, they fear they will lose their adoptive parents as well. This often permeates how they handle their relationship with their adoptive parents. This can be manifested through destructive behaviors to test the permanence of the relationship. That is, will they stick with me even through poor behavior? The other scenario often seen is the "goody-goody" adoptee who is too fearful to challenge or step out of line for fear of being rejected by the adoptive parents.

Through openness, the task of individuation is more successfully accomplished in its incremental way, reaching its peak during the typically difficult adolescent years. Adolescence then can be a more positive experience for the entire family, as grief and identity issues have been dealt with over time.

And, Now, the Children

It is fitting and appropriate to end this book with examples of children's participation in and feelings about their open adoption experiences. We want to share with our readers that many adopted children were asked by their parents to write letters to be included here, but they were unable to actually write anything because they considered open adoption to be very natural and "no big deal." As a result, they could not think of anything to say. We think that is the most positive statement for open adoption, and our hope is that the children of open adoption will continue to feel that open adoption is natural and "no big deal."

Katherine Dorner, age 10½, shares her sentiments about open adoption and contact with her birthmother over the years:

There are two kinds of adoption. Open and closed adoption. Open adoption is when your family knows things about your birthmother and father, and you get pictures and letters. Closed adoption is where you do not know very much about your birth family. I am adopted and know a lot about my birth family. My birthmother Cindy always sends me a birthday card every year, and I know that she loves me. Cindy did not give me up for the sake of giving me up. She gave me up because she loves me. If she had kept me it would have been hard for both of us. My parents love me very much and don't give me any special favors because they think Cindy will come and take me away from them. I am treated like a normal kid. I consider myself special in a certain way because in addition to my mom and dad's family, I have an extra set.

Bree Clark, age 10, describes what he perceives as the benefits of openness:

It feels neat—You get to learn about your ancestry and what your nationality is. . . . You can see what your birthparents look like. . . . They [birthparents] can answer any questions you may have about your adoption.

Cara Speedlin, age 10, who has had an ongoing relationship (letters, phone calls, visits) with her birthmother over the years, comments:

When I hear from Liz (birthmother) or get presents, I feel she still loves me a lot. Liz tells me she loves me.

Cara's sister, Stacy, age 12, describes her transition from closed to open adoption:

Before I had contact, I wondered if they (birthparents) were alive, OK, what they looked like, and why I couldn't be with them. They were on my mind often. Now that I know them I don't have to think horrible thoughts. We're really close and good friends. They're special to me. We have a lot in common.

Kirsten Wunsche, age 8, describes her feelings about her ongoing relationship (visitation and correspondence) with her birthparents:

> I'm happy when my mom tells me I have a letter from Tina (birthmother). I say "Oh, boy, can you read it to me." Most of the time Tina sends pictures of her dog. I know by her letters and pictures that she won't forget me. I won't forget her. I know she loves me. She tells me in her letters and on the phone. I know it when she sends me things. Jim (birthfather) gave me a puppy. I love it. The puppy reminds me of Jim.

Jennifer Dorner, age 8, shares her feelings about contact with her birthmother:

> I feel happy about contact with Gloria. It helps me by letting me know how she is doing. I like her to tell me how much she loves me.

Angela Etter, age 11, who has been engaging in visitation with both birthparents since infancy, reflects:

> I don't have to ask questions. I know everything. I like knowing my cousins from my birthfamily. My favorite part about knowing Mary (birthmother) is that I know she loves me as much as I love her. I feel especially good just seeing her. Other adopted kids tell me I'm lucky because they can't see their birthparents. I see Mary and talk with her on the telephone. I like that. I belong to both families, and I love them both. They like each other, too.

And, finally, Cara Morkert, age 8½, demonstrates the "matter of fact," "no big deal" attitude which the majority of the children of open adoption share:

> Being adopted is lucky if you think about it.
> I think I'm pretty lucky to have two mothers and two fathers.
> I really don't think about it very much though. That's all.

RECOMMENDED READING

Arms, Suzanne, *Adoption: A Handful of Hope*, Berkeley, Celestial Arts, 1989 (originally published as *To Love and Let Go*).

Gritter, Jim, editor, *Adoption Without Fear*, San Antonio, Corona Publishing Co., 1989

Halverson, Kaye with Karen M. Hess, *The Wedded Unmother*, Minneapolis, Augsburg Publishing House, 1980

Johnston, Patricia Irwin, *An Adoptor's Advocate*, Ft. Wayne, IN, Perspectives Press, 1984

Kirk, H. David, *Adoptive Kinship*, Toronto, Butterworth & Co., 1981

Kirk, H. David, *Shared Fate: A Theory of Adoption and Mental Health*, New York, The Free Press, 1964

Lifton, Betty Jean, *Lost and Found*, New York, Harper & Row, 1988

Lindsay, Jeanne Warren, *Open Adoption: A Caring Option*, Buena Park, CA, Morning Glory Press, 1987

Lindsay, Jeanne Warren and Catherine Monserrat, *Adoption Awareness*, Buena Park, CA, Morning Glory Press, 1989

Melina, Lois Ruskai, *Raising Adopted Children*, New York, Harper & Row, 1986

Menning, Barbara Eck, *Infertility: A Guide for the Childless Couple*, Englewood Cliffs, NJ, Prentice-Hall, Inc., 1977

Musser, Sandra Kay, *I Would Have Searched Forever*, Plainfield, NJ, Haven Books, 1979

Pannor, Reuben and Annette Baran, "Open Adoption As Standard Practice," *Child Welfare*, New York, Child Welfare League of America, Inc., Volume LXIII, Number 3, May-June 1984

Rappaport, Bruce M., "The Normalization of Adoption," *New Adoption Journal*, Pleasant Hill, CA, Independent Adoption Center, Summer/Fall Edition 1988

Rillera, Mary Jo and Sharon Kaplan, *Cooperative Adoption*, Westminster, CA, Triadoption Publications, 1984

Silber, Kathleen and Phylis Speedlin, *Dear Birthmother*, San Antonio, Corona Publishing Co., 1983

Sorosky, Arthur D., Annette Baran, and Reuben Pannor, *The Adoption Triangle*, San Antonio, Corona Publishing Co., 1989

Verny, Thomas, MD, with John Kelly, *The Secret Life of the Unborn Child*, New York, A Delta Book, 1981

Wishard, Laurie and William Wishard, *Adoption: The Grafted Tree*, San Francisco, Cragment, 1979

Books for Children

Girard, Linda Walvoord, *Adoption is For Always*, Niles, IL, Albert Whitman & Co., 1986

Krementz, Jill, *How It Feels To Be Adopted*, New York, Knopf, 1982

Lifton, Betty Jean, *I'm Still Me*, New York, Bantam Books, Inc. 1981

Livingston, Carole, *Why Was I Adopted?* Secaucus, NJ, Lyle Stuart, Inc., 1978

Nerlove, Evelyn, *Who Is David?* New York, Child Welfare League of America, 1985

Sly, Kathleen O'Connor, *Becky's Special Family*, Corona, CA, Alternative Parenting Publications, 1985